Apress Pocket Guides

Apress Pocket Guides present concise summaries of cutting-edge developments and working practices throughout the tech industry. Shorter in length, books in this series aims to deliver quick-to-read guides that are easy to absorb, perfect for the time-poor professional.

This series covers the full spectrum of topics relevant to the modern industry, from security, AI, machine learning, cloud computing, web development, product design, to programming techniques and business topics too.

Typical topics might include:

- A concise guide to a particular topic, method, function or framework
- Professional best practices and industry trends
- A snapshot of a hot or emerging topic
- Industry case studies
- Concise presentations of core concepts suited for students and those interested in entering the tech industry
- Short reference guides outlining 'need-to-know' concepts and practices.

More information about this series at `https://link.springer.com/bookseries/17385`.

The Fundamentals of UX Writing

A Practical Guide to Microcopy and Crafting Words That Work

Yael Ben-David

Apress®

The Fundamentals of UX Writing: A Practical Guide to Microcopy and Crafting Words That Work

Yael Ben-David
Kiryat Gat, Southern District, Israel

ISBN-13 (pbk): 979-8-8688-2349-7
ISBN-13 (electronic): 979-8-8688-2350-3
https://doi.org/10.1007/979-8-8688-2350-3

Managing Director, Apress Media LLC: Welmoed Spahr
Acquisitions Editor: James Robinson-Prior
Development Editor: James Markham
Coordinating Editor: Gryffin Winkler

Cover image by eStudioCalamar

Distributed to the book trade worldwide by Springer Science+Business Media New York, 1 New York Plaza, New York, NY 10004. Phone 1-800-SPRINGER, fax (201) 348-4505, e-mail orders-ny@springer-sbm.com, or visit www.springeronline.com. Apress Media, LLC is a Delaware LLC and the sole member (owner) is Springer Science + Business Media Finance Inc (SSBM Finance Inc). SSBM Finance Inc is a **Delaware** corporation.

For information on translations, please e-mail booktranslations@springernature.com; for reprint, paperback, or audio rights, please e-mail bookpermissions@springernature.com.

Apress titles may be purchased in bulk for academic, corporate, or promotional use. eBook versions and licenses are also available for most titles. For more information, reference our Print and eBook Bulk Sales web page at http://www.apress.com/bulk-sales.

Any source code or other supplementary material referenced by the author in this book is available to readers on GitHub (https://github.com/Apress). For more detailed information, please visit https://www.apress.com/gp/services/source-code.

If disposing of this product, please recycle the paper

To my husband Josh who puts up with my crazy

Table of Contents

About the Author

Yael Ben-David Once upon a time, I left my family home outside Washington, D.C., to study in London, Tel Aviv, Russia, Pennsylvania, and New York. Then, BA in hand, I moved to Israel alone, at the age of 22. It seemed like a good idea at the time.

Unenchanted with journalism, I checked out neurobiology, but a master's degree and PhD later, discovered that wasn't my thing either. So I married, had three kids, and landed my first job as a UX writer for a genetics product.

I felt too old to look for something entry level but also had spent so long in academia that I didn't have much professional experience in anything employable to show for myself. A niche role, requiring a cross of professional writing skills and advanced knowledge of genetics, seemed like a perfect fit. And indeed it opened the door to everything that came next. With credentials in writing and science, I had a foot in the door and then learned UX on the job. In fact, I heard the term "UX" for the first time on this job—and it was love at first sight.

I read and listened to all things UX writing. Blogging, tweeting, attending and then speaking at meetups and conferences, teaching a masterclass, giving courses at colleges, and mentoring juniors along the way.

These days, I'm a UX writer/content design leader who specializes in complex products—think finance, health, legal. I'm passionate about making innovative tech accessible to all people through clear, effective, data-driven copy. Writing my first book, *The Business of UX Writing*, was super fun, so I wrote another! I hope you enjoy it.

Acknowledgments

Thank you to James Robinson-Prior at Apress for giving me a chance to write this book; Noa Morag at Reichman University and Dan Kohen-Vacs at Holon Institute of Technology for letting me teach the course this book is based on; and Andy Welfle who reviewed an early manuscript. Thank you to all of the students who've taken my course, provided explicit feedback, and implicit feedback as I watched you work through the exercises and make the course content your own.

Thank you to Kristina Halvorson, Erika Hall, Sarah Winters, Torrey Podmajersky, Kinneret Yifrah, and Roy West who inspired me big time throughout my career and probably don't even know it. And to all of the content designers and thought leaders who have filled my feeds for years and tirelessly produced podcasts and conferences and created spaces from nothing for this field and this community to flourish. The robust collaboration is something special, and it's because this field is full of people who care.

Thank you to mentors whose support in the early days of my UX writing career set the foundation for everything that happened next. I feel like you all know who you are.

Thank you to my husband, Josh, and kids, Maya, Adelle, and Ori, who keep me focused on what matters. No thanks to Boots, who mostly just barks when I'm trying to think.

And most of all, thank you to my grandparents, Lil and Dave Brick, Elaine and Cal Turin, and my parents, Carol and Alan Brick-Turin, to whom I owe my every achievement.

Introduction

In 2019, Kinneret Yifrah published the first "bible" of our field, *Microcopy: The Complete Guide.* I remember sitting on my front porch, with a coffee on a weekend morning. I'd been in my first professional UX writing role ever for about a year and a half, with a very fake-it-til-you-make-it strategy, desperate for something more concrete to hold onto. But there weren't many people around to learn from (including zero UX writers at my company), and this reference guide gave me confidence. I was the first and only UX writer at the company, so people looked to me for answers, and I looked to Yifrah's book. (Back then, we were all UX writers—content designers came later.)

The same year, Torrey Podmajersky published *Strategic Writing for UX.* Just as I was starting to feel like I had a handle on the basics, Podmajersky provided the next stepping stone. I was ready to level up and voila—the next steps on the path to my professional growth were laid out before me. So I read that book and then attended conferences because the latest conversations were coming faster and hotter than books could keep up with. (In 2025, I was honored to be asked to review the second edition of Podmajersky's book, so how's that for full circle!)

It's been six years since those classics came out, and our field has been on one hell of a rollercoaster ride. We've gone from individual, isolated practitioners to finding community. We've gone from spotty research to collaborative breakthroughs. We've gone from a complete user focus to a more holistic approach that sees business stakeholders as powerful collaborators. We saw companies finally "get it" and hire UX writers, then we saw growth into content designer roles, maturing into orgs that needed content design managers...then we went through massive layoffs. Multiple, painful waves. Companies smiled and nodded and said they valued our impact on the bottom line, and then they let us go first when it was time to downsize. According to a top-notch UXCC survey, most were hired back within about a year elsewhere, but it was a tumultuous time.

And then...AI appeared. People claimed GenAI would replace us. We quickly understood that it could not. We took some time to develop prompt engineering skills and started to join teams again. I admit, at first, we were caught off guard. We instinctively became defensive and instead of focusing on how to leverage the tool, mostly shouted from rooftops and soapboxes about how it can't replace us anyway, so whatever, who cares, leave us alone, etc. But then we took the time to process and think together, and get our hands dirty trying it out, and discovered what it can offer us and what we can offer it, and what started as an almost embarrassing hiccup became the start of a beautiful new era.

It's been a lot. Sometimes it feels like we can't catch our breath. Sometimes it feels like we need a hot minute to sit down, regroup, and think through what we've been through and how the landscape has changed, including but not limited to GenAI—both the hype and the reality.

I think about this book as that deep breath. A next-generation "bible." A pause in the crazy journey to collect our thoughts and reassess best practices because we're smarter and more experienced now. So much of the foundations published five, ten, and more years ago still hold true, while others need updating, and some things we know now weren't even vague ideas back then. Let's see where we're up to and go from there.

CHAPTER 1

Microcopy 101

Back when no one had heard of UX writers, someone would ask what I do for a living, and I knew I had an elevator-pitch-worth of attention span to explain. My go-to cocktail party one-liner was: "*When you open an app...the words you see on the screen...I write them.*"

Let's break that down.

Words of the User Experience

"*When you open an app...the* ***words*** *you see on the screen...I write them.*" All the words that guide users within a product to help them interact with it. That includes microcopy, transactional emails, SMS, push notifications, alt text, chatbots, the words of voice interfaces, and more. If you want to know how important the words are in an app, imagine interacting with an interface without them...I feel like a simple registration form before and after words makes the point.

Y. Ben-David, *The Fundamentals of UX Writing*, Apress Pocket Guides,
https://doi.org/10.1007/979-8-8688-2350-3_1

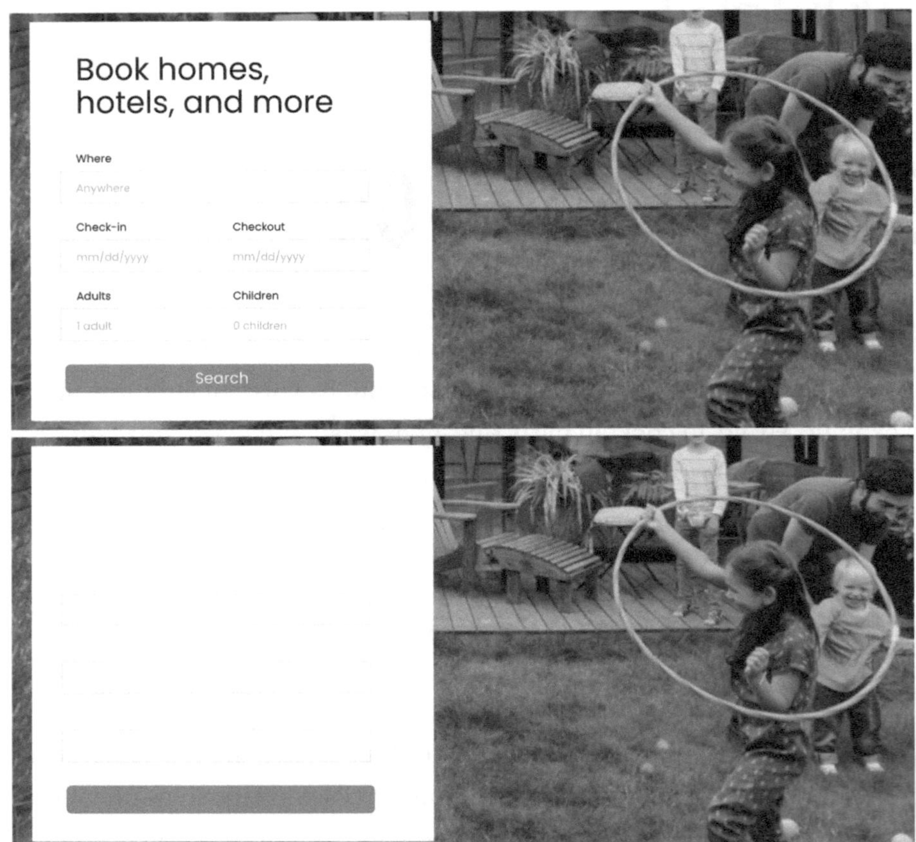

Figure 1-1. *It's essentially impossible to use digital products without copy. Apps don't have value without words*

This isn't just true for digital interfaces. Take my car dashboard, for example:

Figure 1-2. *Sometimes one little word can make all the difference. For usability, inclusivity, accessibility, and other considerations, I will always advocate for labels next to icons*

I'll never forget the day an icon lit up and I panicked. I had no idea what it was supposed to be. I pulled over to the side of the highway, which I really would rather not have, and started flipping through a gazillion-page manual from my glove compartment. Even without the anxiety of the moment, I never could have navigated that thing. So I started Googling…but it was before image search, and how do you even describe that icon?? After much distress, I understood that I had low air in one of my tires. Not no air, not a flat tire, just a heads up that sooner than later I should pop by a gas station and top up. You know what would have saved me a few (many) gray hairs? A word. Maybe two. What we call in the biz, a label. There is plenty of space in the UI. There's no excuse. They could have written: Low air, Low pressure, Tire low, Tire leaking, Add air, Check tire, the list goes on. I can make the case for and against each of these iterations and trust that the team could have found an awesome fit.

Words make interactions smoother. We UX writers make sure of it.

Product, Not Marketing Copy

OK, so we get that words are critical for user interfaces and words are what we UX writers do. What next?

> *"Actually all the words that guide users within a* ***product*** *to help them interact with it."*

Product words are not marketing words. I've worked with incredibly talented marketing writers who write websites and landing pages, often from the earliest wireframing stages. They write ads according to a million, ever-evolving best practices for a multitude of diverse platforms. Personally, I think the hardest thing they write is taglines. I'm in awe of the mind that whips those up. There's copywriting, and there's also content marketing from blogs and white papers to podcast ads, email campaigns, and so much more. There are a plethora of words to be written in the realm of marketing.

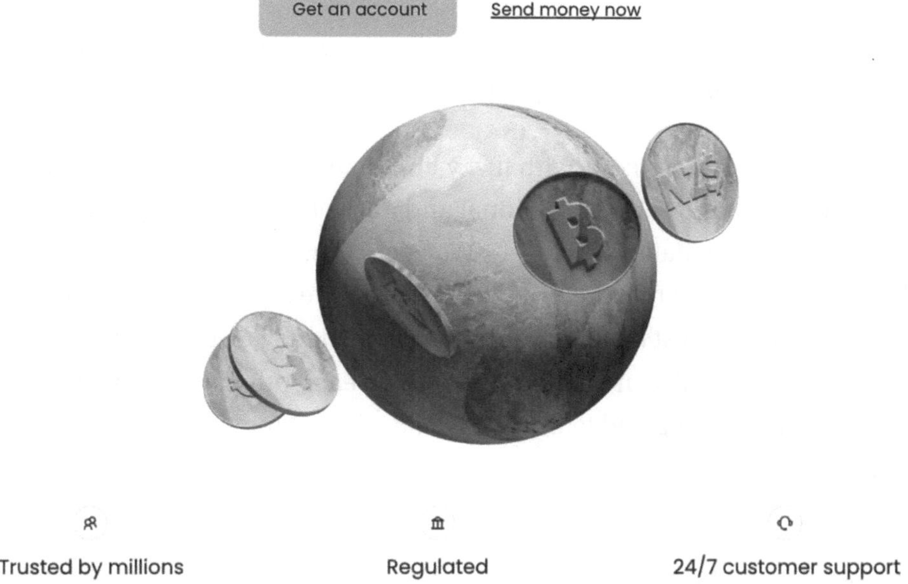

Figure 1-3. *Websites and landing pages are super important and super hard to do well. Marketers write them. They are not UX copy*

Marketers write to pre-users. UX writers write to current users. UX writers write the product experience including when product flows can take users outside the app like to a push notification or transactional email. Even outside the app, users are meeting our copy when they are in a product flow. They are not deciding whether to get the app; they're already using it.

Marketing vs. product copy

	Marketing	Product
Audience	People before they have the product	Users who already have the product
Goal	Sell the product	Achieve users' goals within the product
Example assets	Websites, landing page, digital ads, marketing email campaigns	In-product screens, in-flow push notifications, transactional emails
Purpose	Persuade and attract potential customers	Guide, inform, and assist users within the product
Content focus	Benefits, value propositions, storytelling, brand voice	Actions, instructions, clarity, feedback, error prevention

Figure 1-4. *A crib sheet of the differences between marketing copy and product copy can be helpful*

Of course, there is copy with fuzzy lines like product marketing comms or emails that combine transactional and marketing messaging, and in those cases, we collaborate closely. We each bring our unique skill set to the table because, while there is some overlap, we also each have our area of expertise. The best collaborations happen when we respect and value each other's expertise, not when we try to do each other's jobs. When we focus on listening and learning instead of speaking—that's where the magic happens.

Enabling Interaction

The copy that UX writers write in the product is not just there to look pretty. The copy is how we communicate with the user as they attempt to do a thing.

> *"Actually all the words that guide users within a product to help them **interact** with it."*

UX writing is about interactions. About partnering with the user to do something. It's not a monologue or decorative. We write words to help the user interact by talking them through a process. Buttons, menus, toasts a.k.a. growls (*see note below), notifications, labels, placeholders, validation errors, empty states...these and more elements appear at touchpoints (moments a user interacts with an app, like opening it, receiving a notification, or filling out input fields) where the user is trying to interact with the product. It's a conversation where they "say something" by clicking or tapping or actually talking if it's a voice user interface (VUI), and then we, the product, talk back with the words UX writers write.

*The term "toast" is originally from the Android design guidelines (and later Material Design) and is called that because toast notifications pop in and out of the screen like sliced bread in a toaster. I love that! So cute. Except when I was teaching a group of non-Americans who when *they* say "toast" mean "grilled cheese sandwich"; what Americans call "toast" they call "dry bread" (which is fair). In case you thought localization considerations aren't ubiquitous, they are. Translating for culture references and contexts is the difference between understanding and alienating, between me telling a joke while teaching a class and no one laughing, which is sad. These non-native English speakers, for whom "popping toast" was not intuitive, preferred "growl," named after Growl, a popular early-2000s macOS app that showed pop-up alerts in the corner of the screen, and the name stuck for that style of notification.

Microcopy Is a Superpower

Microcopy is worth getting right because it is *cheap, everywhere,* and incredibly *powerful.*

Cheap (lowering the threshold for revenue when measuring ROI)
Briefly, successful businesses make more money than they spend. The money they bring in is revenue, the money they spend is investment, and the ratio between them is the return on investment, or ROI. The ways to raise your ROI are to make more money or spend less money. When you have a cheap tool to leverage, like microcopy, that's promising for your ROI—you can invest a little and still get out a lot.

Take, for example, a homemade sign drawn with markers on poster board, advertising a yard sale, showing prices, and pointing to where to pay. That copy costs pennies to create, and in return, the yard sale hopefully makes much more than that in revenue.

Figure 1-5. *Words can have a powerful impact on user behavior while costing very little to write and serve*

In a digital context, we have choices: we can guide users through an interaction by leveraging beautiful design, advanced technological solutions, and any number of other expensive solutions. Or we can use words. Microcopy will always be the cheapest solution. It might not be a perfect solution, it might not be elegant, it may feel hacky. But it can get the job done for a lot less investment, and that's a win. Of course, we can also merge approaches, which is probably going to get you the best overall return on investment. Use some design tweaks, some tech upgrades, and a lotta word magic to get the best job done.

I'll give you an example of when words alone did all the heavy lifting. Once, I was working on a flow in a financial app, and for whatever reason, we had to add some information to an already somewhat complicated table of line items. The designer created something elegant that incorporated the new information perfectly. Separately, I tried adding the information using only words without changing the visual design at all. Then, together, we went to get estimates from engineering. The copy solution would save us thousands. It would cost literally half to implement than changing the design. It wasn't perfect, but it was worth it.

It's everywhere you look, no matter what

You can't get away from words. They are absolutely everywhere you look, on and offline. The words are going to be there whether you like it or not, so you might as well get them right. To get them right, start by following best practices. Understand the research and heuristics—mental shortcuts or rules of thumb that people use to make decisions or solve problems quickly and efficiently, without having to carefully analyze every detail; not guaranteed to be perfect but often help us arrive at a good enough answer fast. Understand the product and the user and the business. Don't ignore the words because if you don't do them well, you're doing them poorly. There's no neutral—those are the only options.

I'll never forget the impact a single word had on me on a menu at a restaurant. It's a restaurant outside the United States where a lot of American expats dine. We Americans are used to tipping in restaurants. Always. This restaurant decided to use a different model and wrote on the bottom of the menu, "[We are] proudly a no tipping establishment. Prices include service." If that's all it had said, I would have tipped anyway. Like, I see what you're saying, but also, nope. That's not how I roll. But then they added one more word. "Seriously." Somehow, that drove it home for me. That one word changed my behavior. That one word cost nothing extra to print and resulted in the user, me, taking a completely different action.

There were going to be words on that menu no matter what, but the copy was done well and resulted in an interaction that the user, product, and business all took as a win.

Figure 1-6. *User experience copy is everywhere—not just in digital products*

Powerful on both sides of the scale

Microcopy is powerful for two reasons: it both makes money and saves money. More on this in my first book, *The Business of UX Writing*, but for now, take my word for it. Microcopy can do big things.

There you have it! That's microcopy in a nutshell. Now, let's dig into how we write microcopy well.

CHAPTER 2

Best Practices

According to Oxford Languages, best practices are "commercial or professional procedures that are **accepted** or prescribed as being correct or **most effective**."

According to the Cambridge Dictionary, best practices are "a working method or set of working methods that is officially **accepted** as being the **best** to use in a particular business or industry, usually described formally and in detail."

According to Wikipedia, "A best practice is a method or technique that has been **generally accepted** as superior to alternatives because it tends to **produce superior results**."

I see two themes: best practices have **consensus**, and they produce **better results**. I purposely drew from general references because best practices as a paradigm are definitely not UX writing-specific. Every field has its own best practices, and UX writing is no different in that sense. As everywhere, best practices in UX writing are guidelines, heuristics, that practitioners agree tend to produce better results if followed most of the time.

Best practices in UX writing come from:

Common sense, since we're writing conversations with humans and we writers are humans. A best practice of "be kind" wouldn't surprise anyone. Obviously, words that are kind, we can all agree, will make for a better experience.

Y. Ben-David, *The Fundamentals of UX Writing*, Apress Pocket Guides,
https://doi.org/10.1007/979-8-8688-2350-3_2

Trial and error is where we put content out into the world and follow up on the results to make smarter decisions next time. For example, trial and error might be different writers for different products putting out title case copy and noticing readers slowing down their progress through flows and then coming to the consensus that avoiding title case is a best practice. At this point, they don't have a whole lot of high-quality data, but they do have a compelling theme. The UX writers might then trial a different case and find that the flow completion rate greatly improves. Trying a thing and seeing where it takes you is a perfectly acceptable way to arrive at a guideline. If the same themes are being concluded by multiple practitioners in multiple contexts, consensus around a new heuristic will emerge.

Testing is similar to trial and error, but trial and error has more general takeaways that are more widely applicable to products and use cases other than where the trial took place. This is in contrast to testing, which gives us more specific takeaways and is also more convincing as the metrics tend to be more solid. For example, a company might test actionable vs. descriptive copy on a button at a critical touchpoint in a product flow. Say, comparing the verb "Add" with the noun "Cart." The company would then carefully monitor clickthrough rates and other metrics to determine the success or failure of each approach. When they're done with the test, whatever they find will have strong data to back it but also might be applicable only to specific, similar touchpoints in similar contexts.

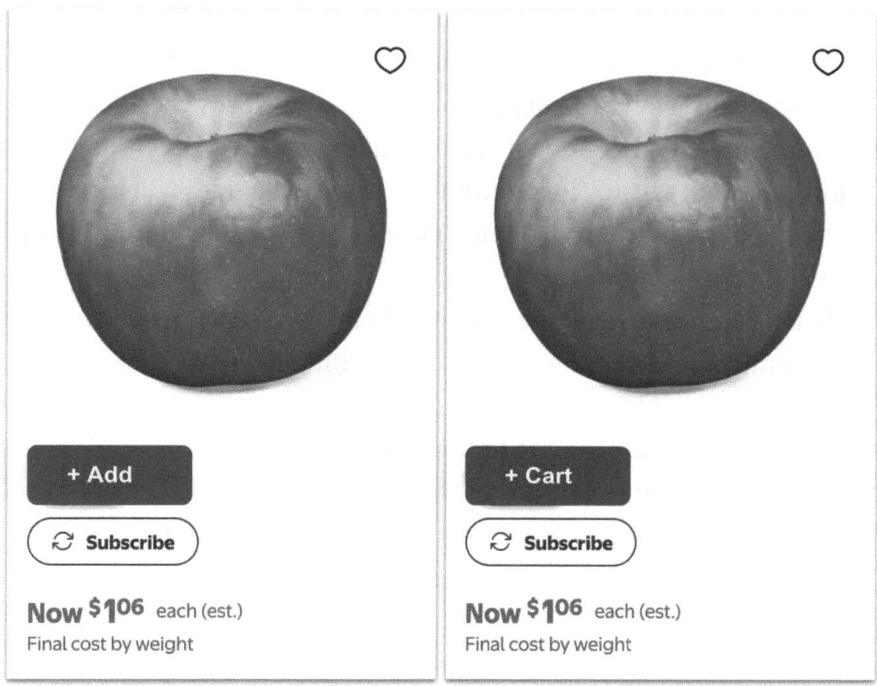

Figure 2-1. *Testing copy is a great way to get to data-informed decisions. Remember to include a control and that you can test more than just one or two options at a time if you have enough users for statistical significance. (I once heard from a UX writer at Booking.com that they had so much traffic that they were able to A/B test in hours and get statistically robust results! This can also take weeks...or months.)*

If they conclude here that the action-oriented copy performed better than the descriptive copy, it's not clear whether that would apply in a non-ecommerce product, or in a product with a more playful voice, or in a million other scenarios. Testing usually has more resources invested because the insights have the potential for big results, but there's a trade-off between how much more credible the results are and how much less widely applicable they are, which is why we want to learn from both trial and error and testing. Get the best of both worlds.

Consensus—Does the UX content community agree? We can change our minds, and that's OK. As we live and learn, we need to be flexible, and as consensus evolves, best practices evolve. Curiosity is critical for maintaining the integrity and efficacy of our field. Especially through trial and error and testing, for a multitude of reasons, tides will turn, and opposite hypotheses will prove true. It's on us to have the humility to shift consensus accordingly.

What are some current best practices in the world of UX writing? What rules of thumb can we use as guidance for writing effective microcopy? Remember, we're looking for best practices that have **consensus** because they are accepted as **producing better results** than if we didn't adhere to them. These are shortcuts, go-tos that will often make your work more efficient. But they won't always be right. They're not fail-safes, and we'll talk about when, why, and how to break them, just as soon as we get through learning what they are.

Clear, Concise, and Helpful

"Clear, concise, and helpful" was first described, as far as I'm aware, by a team at Google in 2017. Watch the talk: How Words Can Make Your Product Stand Out (Google I/O '17). They shared the progression through iterations as they rewrote a piece of copy that was not clear, concise, or helpful, to the point where it was clear but long, then clear and concise but not particularly actionable, to the final version which was clear, concise, and helpful.

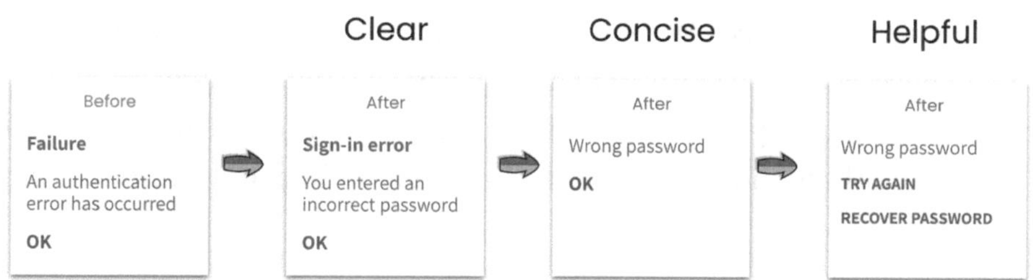

Figure 2-2. *Making sure the copy is clear and concise and helpful all at the same time can take multiple iterations, but it's worth it. See the publicly available video at* `https://www.youtube.com/watch?v=DIGfwUt53nI&ab_channel=GoogleforDevelopers`

This might seem like the most intuitive best practice out there, but it's actually quite a challenging balance to strike. Each element separately—clear, concise, helpful—is pretty obvious for a professional writer. But in an effort to write copy more clearly, you are likely to end up using more words and be less concise. In an effort to be more concise, you run the risk of being so brief you're practically cryptic, and you compromise on being helpful. Adhering to all three pillars at the same time is where the magic lies.

An Important Note About "Concise"

Concise does not (just) mean short. It means giving the user everything they need and nothing more. Every word on the screen should carry its weight. They all need to earn their real estate. There shouldn't be an arbitrary word limit, but all the words that want in need to prove themselves. For example, at the end of a flow that enables a flight tracker, I get the following copy:

"We are ~~now~~ tracking the ~~requested~~ flight. The flight to NRT is expected to depart at 19:00 and arrive at 13:25 local time. We will notify you in case of a change in the flight's schedule. The data will only be stored and available on this device." Without arbitrarily imposing a word limit, I can straight away see three words that are not carrying their weight. "Now," "requested," and "flight's" contribute no value. I am not able to understand anything thanks to those words that I could not understand without them.

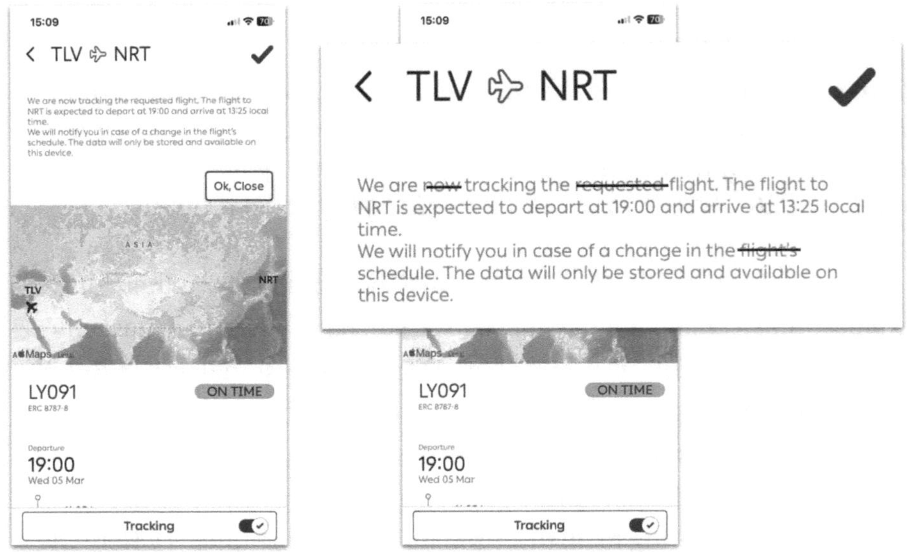

Figure 2-3. *Screenshots from an airline's app show the last touchpoint in an "enable flight tracker" flow. The copy could be more concise*

When I give this exercise to students, they tend to catch the words that can be easily dropped for contributing no value, but they want to go even shorter so they'll often drop the last sentence, too. The thing is, the last sentence is communicating an actual message and removing that message is a decision unto itself. Removing messaging is not making copy more concise; writing concisely is taking the same messaging and saying it in a tighter way. For some reason, the team has decided to include multiple messages in this element:

1. Confirmation that the feature was enabled
2. Current flight status
3. What to expect from the feature going forward
4. Privacy messaging

It is completely valid for a UX writer to start asking questions about these messages. Why are we including all of them? Is there a reason we're not including an additional message that I think is important? If we've already decided that these are the messages that need to be communicated, are we sure this is the right touchpoint to do that? Is this the right order? How are we defining and measuring success? All of that is important, but it is separate from the best practice of writing concisely. When a student comes to me with a rewrite in which they've removed messaging, I don't tell them their copy isn't an improvement over the original, but I do tell them they haven't done "concise" right and should try again. How can you keep all of the messages and still use fewer words, but also not so few that you've made it harder to understand instead of easier?

Exercise for Practicing Clear and Concise

Take a piece of copy from anywhere. Copy you've written, copy you've seen. Decide whether it's clear but not concise; concise but not clear; both clear and concise; or neither. Then fill in the other versions. In my experience teaching UX writing, true proficiency comes not only when you can do it right, but when you can intentionally do it wrong. Then you have fully mastered the practice and will be able to apply it smoothly, as needed.

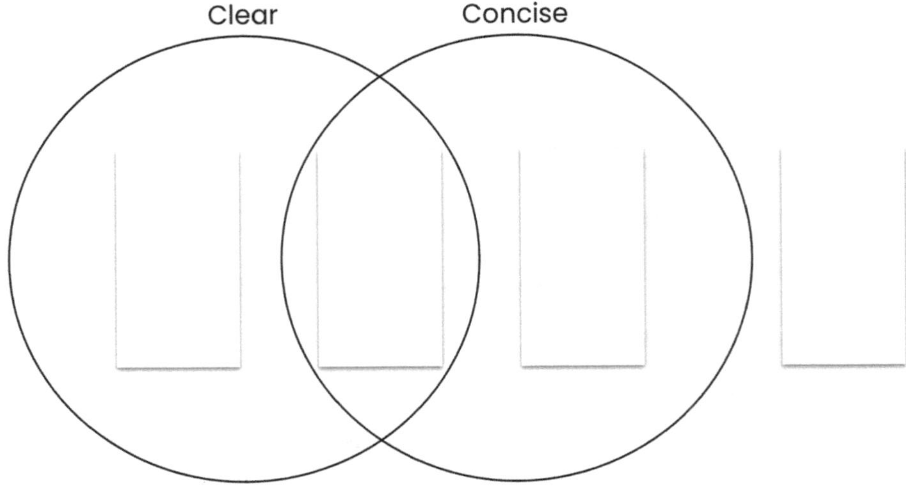

Figure 2-4. *Take a piece of copy. Place it in the Venn diagram where it belongs. Then fill in the three remaining versions. At the end, you'll have the same message written four ways: only clear; only concise; both clear and concise; neither clear nor concise*

I took copy that I saw in the Slack product:

"Notes, to-do's, resources, and more—Now every conversation has a canvas, a place to keep information you don't want to lose in threads."

Notes, to-do's, resources, and more

Now every conversation has a canvas, a place to keep the information you don't want to lose in threads.

Figure 2-5. *A piece of copy in the wild that is neither clear nor concise, is exactly what you need to start working on the exercises in this chapter*

To me, this felt neither clear nor concise. I wanted to rewrite it to be very clear. But first, I had to understand what the copy meant. This actually required me to take several clicks down the progressive disclosure path until I fully understood the feature that was being introduced and was able to explain it in my own words. (See the section "Progressive disclosure, tell an engaging story" later on for more on this.)

However, my new, clear copy ended up being so long that no one would read it. It was super clear—to the zero people who would read it. So really, I'd accomplished nothing.

I tried again, focusing on conciseness. This time, the copy was so tight that it felt like important messaging was missing. And the messaging I did include took superfluous cognitive load to decode. The trick with conciseness is not to say less, unless there are good reasons certain messages shouldn't be included; rather, it's to say what needs to be said in a brief way.

Finally, I came up with a version that felt like a good balance between clear and concise, the best of both worlds without costing too much of either, giving the user the best overall copy possible.

Clear: ***Canvases are a new place to keep info you don't want to lose*** In any Slack conversation you have, you'll find a new "canvas" where you can keep notes, to-dos, resources and more. It's a convenient way to keep track of important information between you and a coworker, like organizing priorities together, and collaborating on action items from a direct message conversation.

Concise: ***Canvas*** A new place to save info from conversations.

Neither clear nor concise: ***Notes, to-dos, resources, and more*** Now every conversation has a canvas, a place to keep information you don't want to lose in threads. Put stuff there you and a colleague might want each other to know after the conversation.

Clear and concise: ***A place to keep info you don't want to lose*** Keep the "canvas" in each conversation for notes, to-dos, resources, and more.

By the way, when I last checked the Slack app in March 2025, instead of the copy I used on the exercise prepared long before then, I saw the updated:

"**Introducing Canvases**—A new way for teams to collaborate, curate, and share information inside of Slack." Definite improvement!

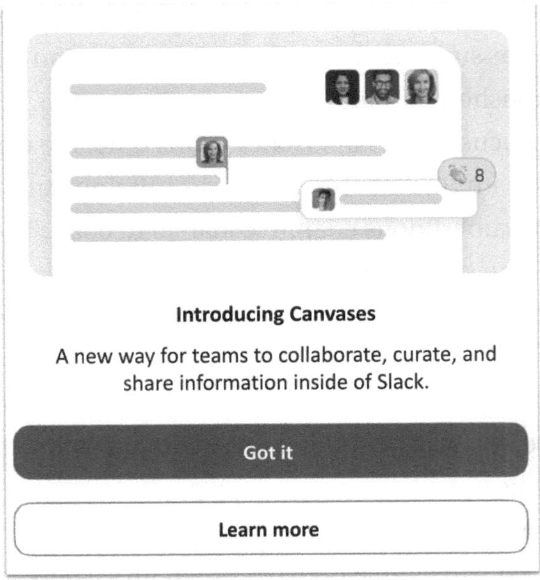

Figure 2-6. *The March 2025 version of the UX copy introducing the Canvases feature is a major improvement over an older version I used to show when teaching about balancing clear and concise*

Writing According to Conventions (Norms)

Using conventions means using the words that are conventional—normal—for the user base. Sometimes these will be intuitive to the UX writer, and sometimes they won't. Either way, using those words is the right thing to do. Users are interacting with offline flows; they are anchored to interactions that existed before your product and continue to exist outside your product, and to be successful, you need to speak like them, not the other way around. Do not reinvent their terms or expect them to learn your version. They won't. (Unless you're like, Apple or Meta. They recontextualize words, and the world adopts their new connotations.)

Here's an example: I was working for a fintech product. I didn't know much about fintech. And that's fine, because UX writers need to be experts in UX writing, not the vertical their product lives in. Otherwise, we'd be very niche, and our careers would be quite the struggle. A good UX writer can work in any vertical and, instead of becoming a subject matter expert, fosters relationships with subject matter experts. So I was writing a flow where a "seller" first **authorizes** funds and then later **captures** funds from a "buyer's" credit line.

I didn't really know what those terms meant, "authorizes and captures," so I sat with experts and walked away thinking, OK, authorize sounds to me like it basically means "freeze funds," or "hold funds," or "reserve funds." And capture sounds to me like it basically means "process payment," "send funds," or "transfer funds." First, the seller freezes some of the buyer's credit line to be sure the amount will be available for payment after the merchandise is delivered, and then later, to complete the deal, collects the funds that were previously held. Did I use those terms: freeze and collect? Absolutely not. Because those are not the conventions for the seller or buyer user personas. They don't talk like that, based on user interviews and feedback from customer service reps. Users do not expect to see those terms and should not have to reverse engineer or decode my attempts at "intuitive" language (intuitive to whom??) in order to land back at the conventional term they are familiar with. I'd have to use "authorize and capture." (Actually, in the end, we found that while sellers and buyers both use the conventional "authorize," the term "capture" was less intuitive to buyers, and so we used "authorize and process payment" to be inclusive and intuitive for both personas.)

Another reason to stick to existing conventions is to protect your credibility. If I'm writing about payment processing and don't use the terms that are normal and expected in that space, I look like I don't belong. Who would trust their money to a financial product like that, who clearly doesn't "get it"? Balancing convention and intuitiveness can be tricky, but with enough user research, content designers can land where the copy needs to be.

Consistency for the Sake of Clarity

Consistency is something we expect from people and businesses we interact with in real life, and without necessarily being aware of it, we expect the same from digital experiences as well. (I recommend *The Man Who Lied to His Laptop* by Clifford Nass for a deep dive on the human expectation that digital interactions feel like human interaction when it comes to product language.)

"Managing expectations" is a thread that flows throughout all of the user experience work that we do, including sticking to conventions discussed earlier, because those are the words that users expect to hear, and continues with consistency—continuing to communicate in the way your users have gotten used to and now expect.

Consistency can mean using the same **language** again and again. A lot of brands have an internal glossary of sorts so that when there are multiple ways to say one thing, all teams can align to the same term and give the user a consistent experience.

Consistency can also be in the **behavior** of elements, but that would lie more in the designer's jurisdiction. (When can users expect to meet drop-downs vs. radio buttons vs. checkboxes... or where on the screen do certain widgets tend to live, and things like that.)

Consistency can also mean consistency in **structure** and **casing**.

Structure: The Setup Is As Important As the Words

I once wrote a progress bar where we started by labeling each step, in a vacuum: If this were the only step in the world, what would be the best name for it? We took each screen in the flow and gave it the very best title we could think of. But then, we stepped back and looked at the step titles as a set, and they were not in the same structure. One was an imperative. One was descriptive. One was a single word, while the others were quite a few more. Starting with the very best titles we could was the right move, but then zooming out to look at the copy as a whole experience was important, too.

We ended up rewriting them to hold onto the best of what we could from the first iteration while also conforming to some kind of template. In the end, all three steps had more than one word and were phrased in actionable, second person language.

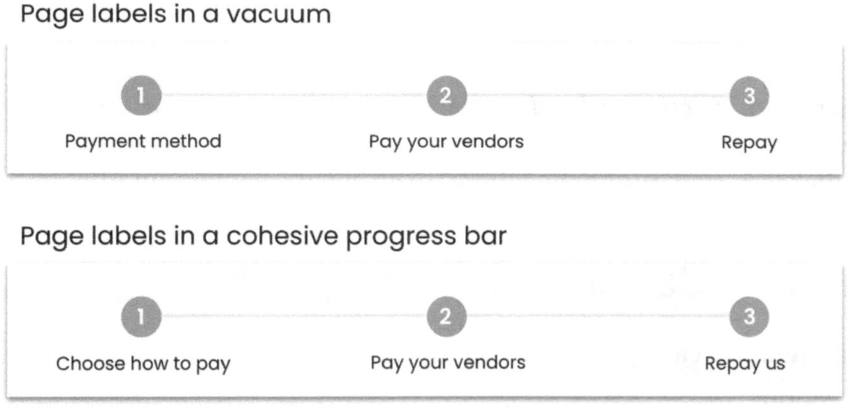

Figure 2-7. *A process bar with a consistent structure meant each step's label had more than one word, was in second person, and used actionable language*

Here's another example:

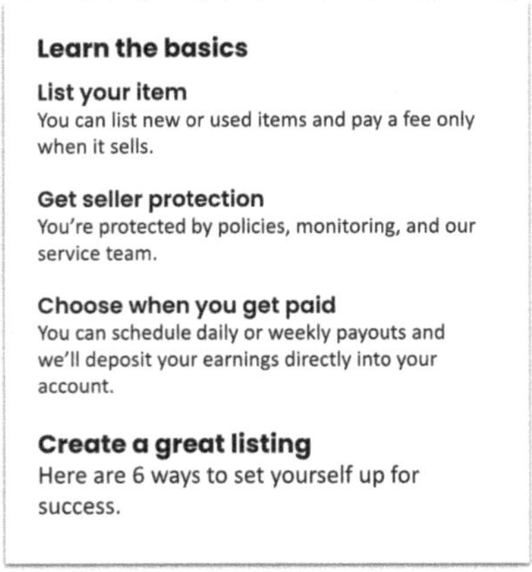

Learn the basics

List your item
You can list new or used items and pay a fee only when it sells.

Get seller protection
You're protected by policies, monitoring, and our service team.

Choose when you get paid
You can schedule daily or weekly payouts and we'll deposit your earnings directly into your account.

Create a great listing
Here are 6 ways to set yourself up for success.

Figure 2-8. *Section titles that start "Learn" and "Create" in one font size, and subsection titles that start "List," "Get," and "Choose" in a smaller font size, make the whole thing extra easy to navigate*

Choosing Casing and Sticking with It

Consistency in casing is important for credibility, too. Without it, you just look sloppy.

Sentence case is easiest to read because we are used to it and it has become the most common case in most apps.

Title Case Also Has a Time and a Place (Like Newspaper Headlines Where It Originated), and Many Apps Use It in Certain Elements. Start Case Is Similar, But It Capitalizes The First Letter Of Every Word And Is Rarely Used Because It Slows The Reader Down.

ALL CAPS FEELS AGGRESSIVE TO MOST USERS SO IT IS ALMOST NEVER USED; OCCASIONALLY YOU WILL SEE IT, AND FOR VERY SHORT BUTTONS OR MENU ITEMS, IT CAN WORK.

CamelCaseIsForHashtags.

(Ya see what I did there?)

Now I'm not suggesting you choose a case and use it for every single string* across the entire product experience. But within a level of hierarchy, or element, or other single context, I would expect consistent casing. For example, all buttons in all caps. Or all link text in sentence case. While we will talk about when, why, and how to break best practices because sometimes that is the right thing to do, when it comes to consistency in casing within a defined context, I've never seen an exception that made sense. Even huge brands don't get this right all the time—a reminder that the giants also make mistakes, also have short circuits in communication, legacy code, and knowledge transfer gaps with personnel turnover.

*"Strings" are a data type used to represent text: a sequence of characters (letters, numbers, symbols, or spaces). You can think of a string as a line of text enclosed in quotes. It's what developers call our microcopy when they code it.

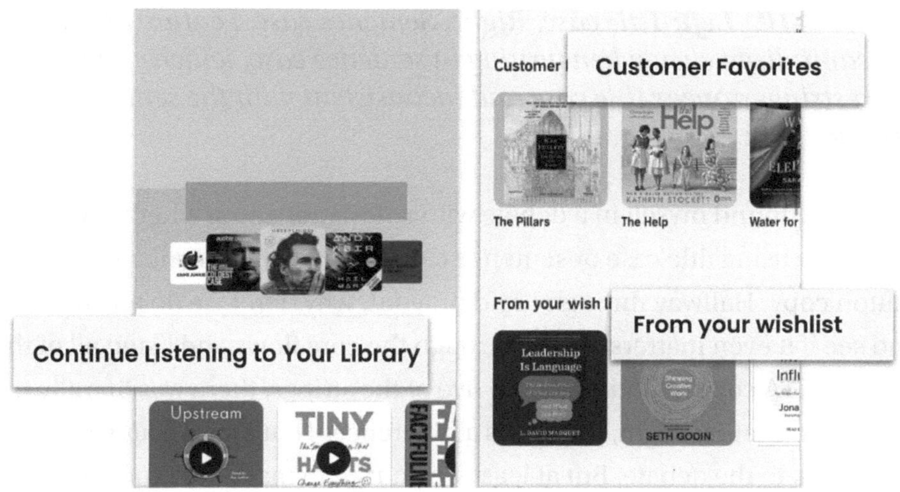

Figure 2-9. *Section titles are all in the same level of hierarchy and therefore should be written in the same case, whatever that case is. Two titles in title case and the third in sentence case feels a bit off*

I should add, the case you're in doesn't actually always matter. For example, a one-word string, like the button text, "Start", is written exactly the same way in sentence case and title case. A two-word menu item in sentence case, where the second word is a proper noun, will also look identical to title case. In these cases (ha!), no one will ever know what case you thought you were writing in, and it won't matter.

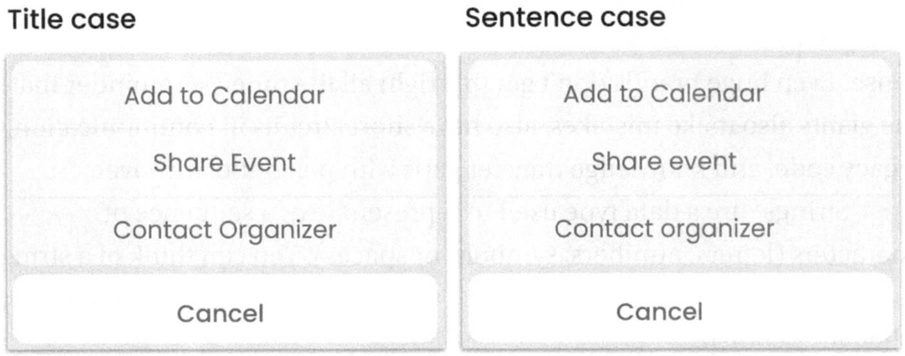

Figure 2-10. Left*: Title case.* ***Right****: Sentence case. Feature names are capitalized even when writing in sentence case, which can make short strings appear title case and inconsistent with the sentence case around them*

I once found myself in a debate with a designer about whether we should be using title case or sentence case on our calls to action (CTAs)/ button copy. Halfway through I said timeout, why don't we do an audit and see if it even matters. I went through the core flows and listed all of the existing CTA copy in both cases. In five of the strings, there was literally no difference at all. In eight, there was a difference. That's significant so we went back to the debate. But at least we paused to make sure there was a point in debating at all. (I argued to leave the existing title case because it was a convention at the time in the industry and didn't seem worth the investment for any marginal improvement switching over to sentence case might provide—I always had so many back burner project that if a sprint had bandwidth for copy changes, there were 86 things I would have preferred to push forward.)

Avoid Jargon, Idioms, Metaphors, Similes, and Slang

You might think jargon sounds fancy or extra professional, that metaphors sound erudite, and that slang makes you sound cool. The truth is, they make your content harder to consume, and the trade-off is not worth it.

Figure 2-11. *Jargon and slang are often more alienating than they're worth, even if they are an opportunity to express your voice*

Jargon is specialized words used by a particular profession or group.

Idioms are expressions whose meaning can't be understood from the literal words ("spill the beans").

Metaphors are a comparison saying one thing *is* another ("time is money").

Similes are a comparison using *like* or *as* ("as fast as lightning").

Slang is informal, often trendy words used in casual speech.

Jargon, idioms, metaphors, similes, and slang have varying degrees of familiarity across ages, geography, cultures, and levels of education. Even within a profession, jargon does not necessarily cross levels of experience, cultures, or geographies. Why use language that alienates and excludes certain users when you can use plain language to include them? It's the right thing to do as well as opening new markets that would now have access to your product.

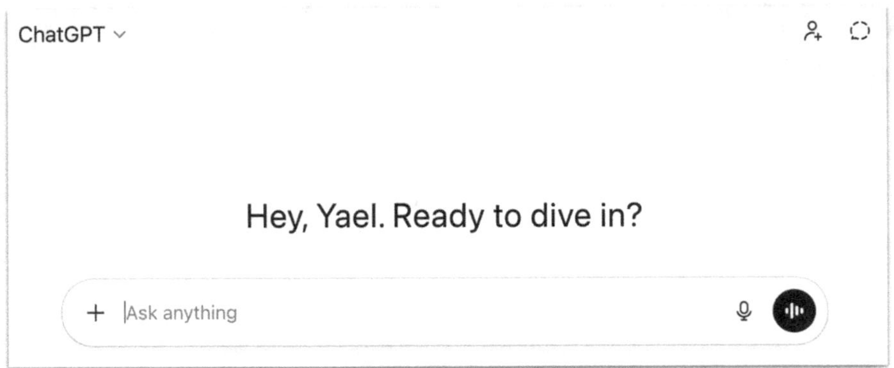

Figure 2-12. *Is there any interface being read by a more diverse, global audience right now than ChatGPT? I was shocked they went with idiomatic language. Though perhaps they have so much data on me that this is dynamic text customized precisely and other audiences aren't actually seeing it*

Now, there is an important difference between jargon and technical terms. Jargon usually refers to language that sounds complicated, impressive, or insider-only—sometimes without adding real clarity. Technical terms, on the other hand, exist to be precise. They describe concepts that don't have simple everyday equivalents, so using them actually improves accuracy and understanding within a field.

If I'm writing for a specific professional audience, it is important to use the technical language that they use. Otherwise, the product looks like it doesn't belong in their space. If we can't use the users' conventions, we don't have integrity or sound like we know what we're talking about. We don't come off as trustworthy or credible.

NNGroup published an insightful article where they call out, "Jargon is helpful, however, when it communicates a concept clearly understood by specialized user groups. When expert groups share a common vocabulary, technical jargon can serve as a shortcut in communication. For example, for physicians, 'ventricular tachycardia' is a lot shorter and more precise than 'rapid heart rhythm that arises from improper electrical activity of the heart and starts in the bottom chambers of the heart." And while experts can pack a lot of meaning into their technical terms, they still want to see plain language and simple structures around it. Read the whole NNGroup report at https://www.nngroup.com/articles/plain-language-experts/.

Who Is It For?

Before I started doing research for this book, I always taught my students that avoiding jargon, idioms, metaphors, similes, and slang was about accommodating people from different cultures and levels of education including fluency in the language of the interface. But after diving a bit deeper, I'd add that this best practice is also for the sake of people who have poor working memory, are easily distracted, are slower at reading or processing information, have a very literal understanding of language, are reading in a rush, have learning difficulties, are dyslexic, are autistic, and have anxiety. And honestly, even experts prefer plain language when possible (https://www.nngroup.com/articles/plain-language-experts/). Scope expands on this idea that plain language actually helps more user groups than you might think (https://business.scope.org.uk/how-to-improve-your-writing-with-plain-english/).

How Do You Know You're Doing It Right?

There are tools that can help you determine if you're choosing plain language that makes sense for your users. One I've used is Hemingway (`https://hemingwayapp.com/`). I mostly used it to determine the reading level, but check it out; it can catch and recommend solutions for a number of pitfalls.

The Plain English Campaign offers lots of free resources and guidelines at `https://www.plainenglish.co.uk/free-guides`. They offer a plain English guide for writing forms and many other short documents with easy-to-read guidelines and tips for writing products in a way that will bring in users instead of alienating them.

Even governments have gotten on board and have published legal requirements and guidelines for writing in plain language (see `https://www.digital.govt.nz/standards-and-guidance/design-and-ux/content-design-guidance/writing-style/plain-language`). In the context of ROI—getting sued is bad for business! I recommend you find the relevant readability-related legislation for where you work and align accordingly.

One of the toughest places to use plain language is in legal content, and every product has at least some. I've seen a few approaches for Terms of Use and Privacy Policy-type content. One is every few paragraphs, summing up what's been said, in plain English, like Pinterest does.

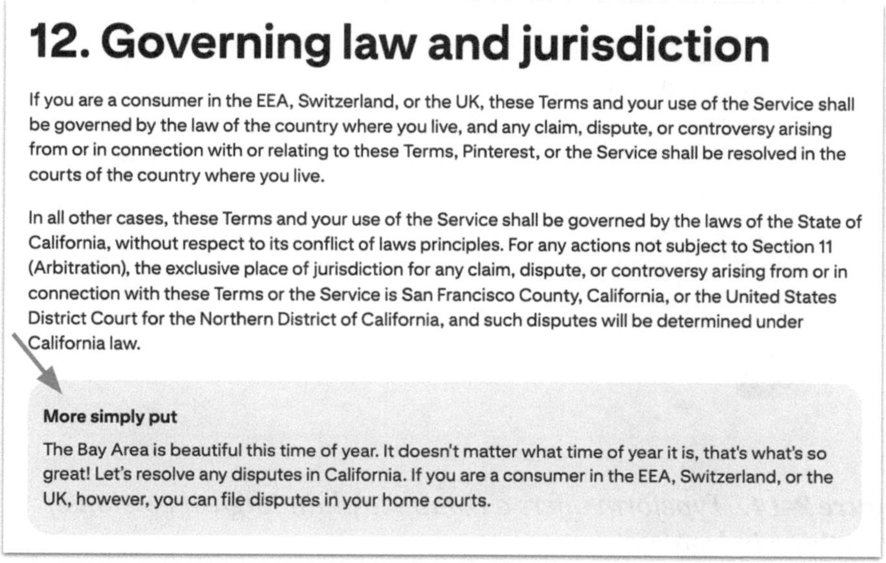

12. Governing law and jurisdiction

If you are a consumer in the EEA, Switzerland, or the UK, these Terms and your use of the Service shall be governed by the law of the country where you live, and any claim, dispute, or controversy arising from or in connection with or relating to these Terms, Pinterest, or the Service shall be resolved in the courts of the country where you live.

In all other cases, these Terms and your use of the Service shall be governed by the laws of the State of California, without respect to its conflict of laws principles. For any actions not subject to Section 11 (Arbitration), the exclusive place of jurisdiction for any claim, dispute, or controversy arising from or in connection with these Terms or the Service is San Francisco County, California, or the United States District Court for the Northern District of California, and such disputes will be determined under California law.

More simply put

The Bay Area is beautiful this time of year. It doesn't matter what time of year it is, that's what's so great! Let's resolve any disputes in California. If you are a consumer in the EEA, Switzerland, or the UK, however, you can file disputes in your home courts.

Figure 2-13. *Pinterest, every few paragraphs of legal text, sums up what's been said in plain English*

Another approach is offering a complete plain English version of everything in legalese like Typeform (with a disclaimer of course that the unintelligible version is the one that counts).

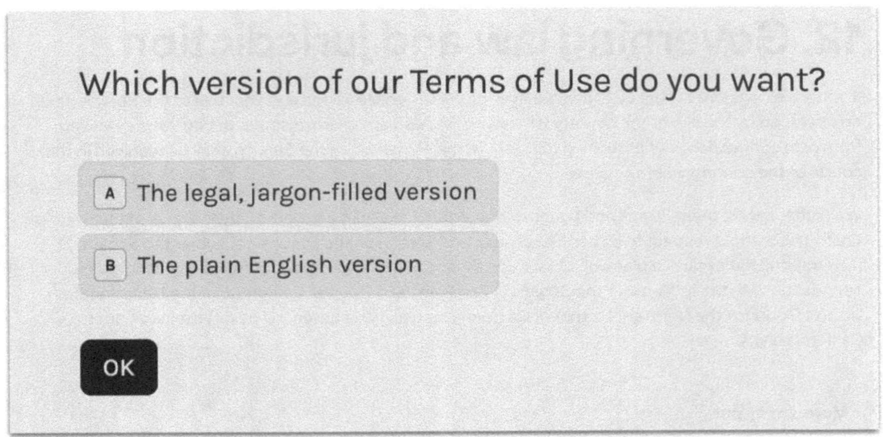

Figure 2-14. *Typeform offers a complete plain English version of everything in legalese*

For more on this, check out content on writing in plain language by Sarah Winters, Ginny Redish, and Caroline Jarrett (start with `https://www.effortmark.co.uk/why-plain-language-and-plain-english-are-different/`).

Device-Agnostic Because Your Users Are All Over the Place

If you're writing for a product that is only available on one type of device, you can skip this section. Many digital products, however, are available on desktop and mobile; and within the world of mobile, multiple types of phones and tablets; and some, as voice interfaces, too. As a general rule of thumb, as a best practice, we want to write one string that works for all devices to save on development costs up front and leave less room for bugs later. That means avoiding terms like "tap" and "swipe," which only work on mobile, not desktop, and "click," "hover," and "drag and drop," which go the other way around.

I've seen cases like "Tap to Call" on the Zappos interfaces on mobile, which breaks this practice, and I'm not sure why. There seem to be easy workarounds that would work on mobile as well as desktop, like just writing "Call" and having the element clickable or "Call us at" with the number, just to name two off the top of my head. It also crossed my mind that perhaps this feature—a shortcut to call from the interface itself—is only available on mobile, which is why the copy within the feature is not device-agnostic. In that case, it's OK as is.

Figure 2-15. *Device-specific language is either only served on that device, or a mistake*

In contrast, for a crypto wallet app I wrote, the whole product was available exclusively on mobile, so I freely and comfortably allowed myself to use mobile-specific language, like "Exchange one crypto for another in a few taps".

Figure 2-16. *When an app is only available on a particular device, then device-specific language is appropriate*

If, for some reason, it's been decided that for a product or feature that is available on multiple device types, you want to use device-specific language, you'll maintain multiple versions of the string in the code and serve each according to the respective device a given user is experiencing. Because reading "pinch to zoom" on a non touch-screen desktop isn't awesome.

Dynamic text is copy that changes depending on what's going on for the user. And it can help make great experiences! But as a solution for getting around device-agnostic language, it doesn't seem worth it. Maintaining dynamic text just so you can serve "click" on desktop and "tap" on mobile feels like a waste of resources. Use better copy to keep your investment low.

My favorite case of dynamic text is when the same state appears at different points in time. For example, if I'm sent a money transfer and don't accept it right away, like in the Bit app. Then it's much more worth it. The string changes from "...await[ing] approval for another 3 days" to

"...another 2 days" to "...until tomorrow", and that's pretty cool. Of course, they could have gone with the static "...until [date]" if they'd wanted to, but the dynamic experience feels better.

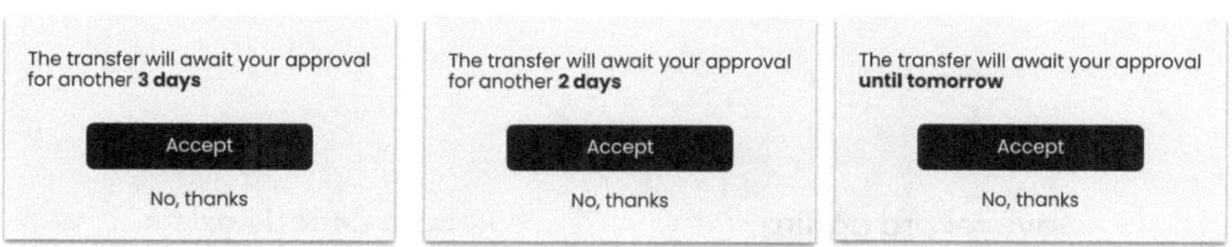

Figure 2-17. *Dynamic text is when the same state appears at different points in time*

Title-CTA Continuity Because Users Read or Don't

This best practice is based on the assumption that users don't always read everything we write (but some users will at least some of the time). Take a pop-up, for example—that's a disruptive experience. The user was doing a thing, and then a window popped up in their face, literally covering what they were in the middle of and are still trying to see. They want that thing gone. So they'll read the title to understand what just happened and then the CTA to make it go away. There are limited use cases where it will be worth it to them to stop and read the body text in between.

That doesn't mean we shouldn't write body text in between! There will be users who need or want it, and we owe it to them. It just means we need to make sure that the one pop-up works for both scenarios—users who read and users who don't. It's actually not that hard.

For example, imagine a user is saving a record, but the record was already previously saved. While it makes perfect sense to say, "Record already exists, are you sure that you want to save this record again? Yes/No", that pop-up won't make as much sense to a user who skips the middle and gets "Record already exists, Yes/No".

However, if we tweak the copy to "Save record again, This record already exists, do you want to save it again? Yes/No", it'll work regardless of whether the user reads all that or skips the middle and ends up with "Save record again, Yes/No".

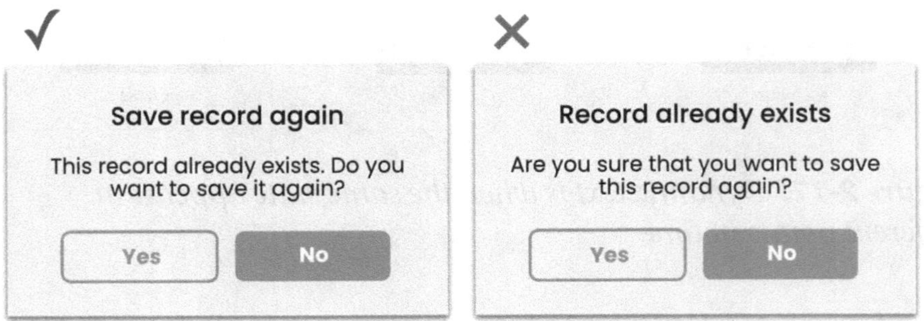

Figure 2-18. *Some users will read your body text, while others won't, and both need to be able to use the app*

The same principle applies to a pop-up that reads "No results found. You haven't created any ads yet. Create Ad"; it'll work regardless of whether the user reads all that or skips the middle and ends up with "No results found. Create Ad".

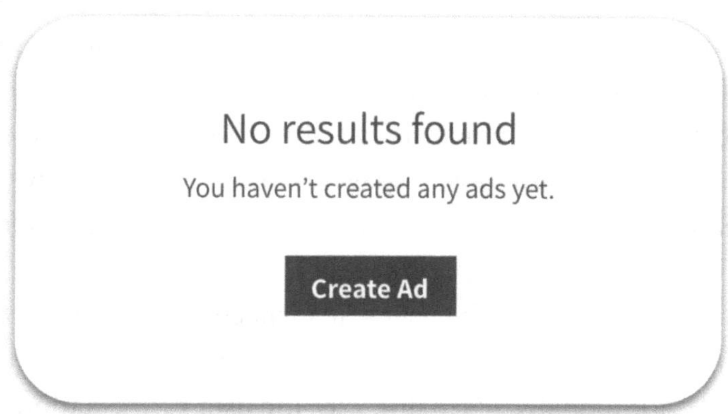

Figure 2-19. *Your title and CTA need to make sense when they are read in a vacuum. Because they will be read in a vacuum by many users, no matter how hard you worked on the copy in between*

Title-CTA continuity means that when you have a title or primary text of any kind, secondary text, and an interactive element, the flow of content consumption needs to work for whichever reasonable combination of the strings different users choose to read.

Actionable CTAs Because Users Want to Do a Thing

If product copy is a conversation with the user, CTAs are their most powerful turn to talk. Anytime they click, tap, or in any way interact with the experience, that's their side of the back-and-forth.

First of all, keep that in mind when deciding whether to write button copy in first or second person. If the title says, "Go to your dashboard for more information", the button would say, "Take me there". The button copy is from the user's perspective because when they click, they talk. It's their turn. The button in this case should not say, "Take you there".

An even safer option is for button copy to be person-ambiguous. Like "Go to dashboard". That can be interpreted as "Hey you, go to your dashboard" or "Bye! I'm off to my dashboard now".

Second, when users interact with a button, it's because they want to do a thing. They want to learn more or pay now or sign out. Whatever it is, it's a verb; therefore, the language on the button should be actionable. Write "Pay now", not "Payment".

This is more in line with the user's headspace and intentions and therefore feels natural and gives them confidence that it really is the right thing to click. Additionally, it's in line with the user's expectations, which means they'll be less anxious and the interaction will feel more organic and comfortable. "Pay now" tells me exactly what's about to happen. "Payment" could be any of a number of steps in the payment process or even just information about the payment process that doesn't move me closer to completing the transaction. Furthermore, based on the assumption that we generally want users to click our buttons, actionable language is more motivating. If it's in their best interest and in our best interest as the business behind the product to get the button clicked, actionable language moves the needle in that direction.

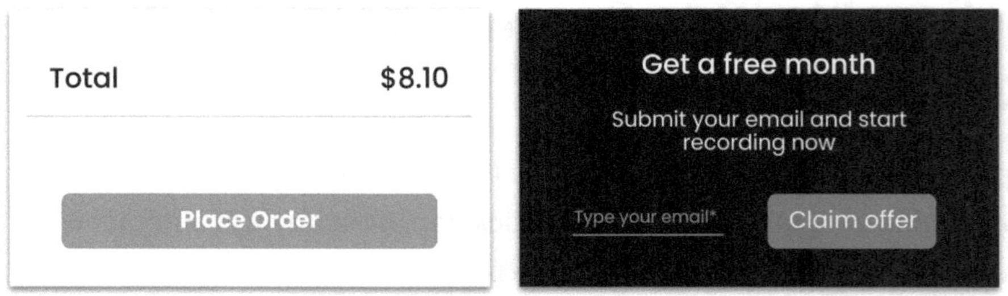

Figure 2-20. *When a user clicks or taps, they're doing a thing. They're taking an action, and the copy should be in line with that vibe*

What about "Done" or "Next", you're thinking. And you're right! These are not actionable. It's possible to rewrite them with imperative verbs. (An imperative verb is a verb used to give a command, instruction, or request. Examples: Stop, Open, Click, Listen, Tell me.) But here's why I think these are acceptable exceptions: They align with the best practice of convention. They perfectly manage expectations of what's about to come next. They still sound like they're coming from the user's mouth and not ours. And most of all, these are actions we don't need to invest in motivating. In the Breaking Best Practices section later, we'll cover another type of exception that's even more juicy.

Frontloading (Whichever Direction That Might Be)

We know that often users read the beginning of a line of text and then stop (`https://www.nngroup.com/articles/f-shaped-pattern-reading-web-content/`). Either they stop reading altogether, or they skip to the next line and read only the beginning of that line too before skipping to the third or, if it's short interactive text instead of long form, just jump to the interaction and click without ever having read more than the first few words of the whole screen. That's why we have to squash our most important message into those first few words. It might come at the expense of some of the most eloquent, articulate, even poetic writing, but if the user doesn't read it, who cares. Whatever we need them to know—tell them first, since you may not get another chance.

That critical message is the action. "Apply in five minutes or less". After that, I might explain about the process, but what I need them to know first and foremost is that right here, right now, we're applying. Say I swap it and write "In only five minutes you can apply" and the user doesn't get past the first few words. They know something only takes five minutes, but what? If I had to choose between them only knowing this is the place to apply or knowing that this place takes five minutes to interact with, you can bet your bottom dollar I'm going with "apply." They would too because that gives them the most critical information, fastest, with the least friction or cognitive load on their side.

The exception to frontloading the action might be frontloading the value prop (value proposition: a clear statement of the benefit a product or service provides to customers). If you're in a context where the user is trying to understand what you offer that others don't, what's so attractive about continuing toward the apply flow for example, the why might need to be answered before the how.

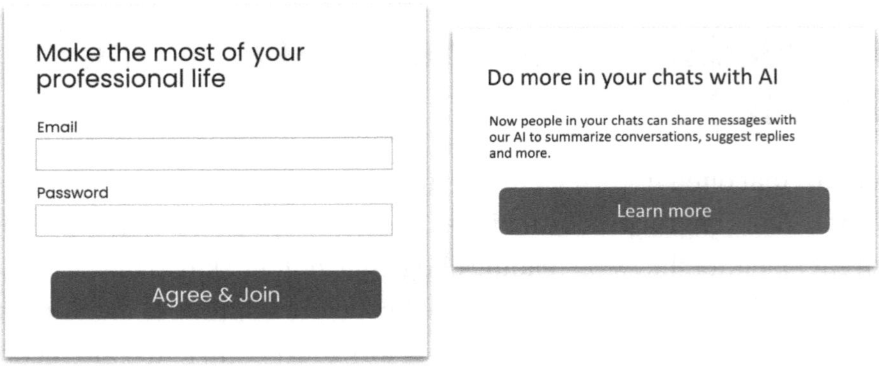

Figure 2-21. *Frontloading value over technicalities can have a powerful impact on user behavior*

LinkedIn is good at this. I don't think I've ever seen them start with the "how"—sign up, log in, enter your email, etc. They frontload "Make the most" so I know whatever comes next is gonna be good stuff (just one of the many versions I've been served, all following the same approach). Following their model means writing "Invest easily when you join" instead of "Join to invest easily". It means choosing "Get advice in 1 business day" over "In 1 business day you get advice".

Do's and don'ts of frontloading	
Do	**Don't**
Start with what or why, e.g., Grow your network	Start with how, e.g., Sign up or log in to start
Start with the most important information, e.g., Get advice fast	Bury the most important information, e.g., Quickly get advice
Assume users will consume only the first words	Write descriptors first, e.g., Now apply
Start with the most important message and use modifiers afterwards, e.g., Apply now	Require users to read the whole string for it to make sense

Figure 2-22. *Follow the general "do's" and "don'ts" of frontloading to increase your copy's impact*

It should go without saying that the "front" in "frontload" depends on the language. In English, for example, frontloading means putting the important stuff all the way on the left; in Hebrew or Arabic, frontloading means putting the important stuff all the way on the right.

Scannable Because Not All Words Need to Be Read

We want to help our users get where they're going as fast as possible (most of the time), and that means them not getting caught up on reading the words we wrote. If we could communicate telepathically, or just zap meaning into their brains without their eyeballs processing the page, that's what we would want to do. As of the writing of this manuscript, the closest we can get to zapping is using copy that can be scanned.

Scannable copy helps users get what they need in seconds, because most people skim screens rather than read carefully. So how do we do that?

For starters, for short text, stick to concise and conventional text. If button text matches user expectations, they'll recognize the shape before they read the words and know what to do before ever reading the action.

And avoid all caps. It was once believed that because all caps mean every letter is in the same shape, as opposed to sentence case where some letters reach up (b, d) and others reach down (g, q), all caps are harder to scan, i.e., recognize before reading. The newer theory is that the reason all caps are read slower is just because people aren't used to it. Either way, sentence case is more scannable.

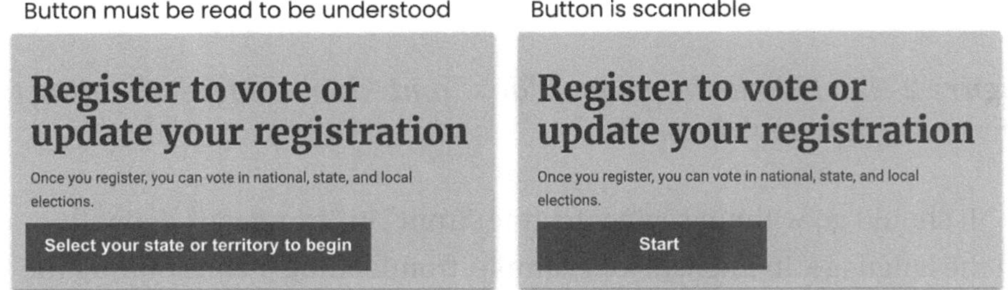

Figure 2-23. *When everything the user needs to know is in the title, I can afford to keep the button short and sweet. No need to compromise best practices like frontloading, scannable, and convention by repeating myself*

For **medium-length** content, use bullet points. They don't actually need to be little dots. Work with your designers, and the bullets functionality can be fulfilled with icons that even further support communication without reading. Bullet points signal when one idea stops and the next begins so that a user can decide halfway through a point that they get it, don't need the rest of the sentence, and are guided intuitively and quickly where to jump next.

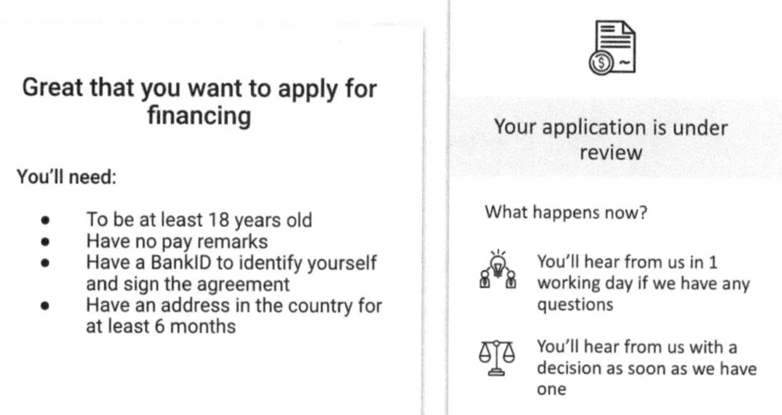

Figure 2-24. *Bullet points are a way to combine the best practices of frontloading and scannable. The synergy is fire*

For **long-form** content, use section titles and subsection titles so users can scan only those, to get the gist up front, and so they can navigate to the parts most relevant for them and start there. No reason to make them dig through a whole post when they need something specific that you indeed offer...if you can get them there.

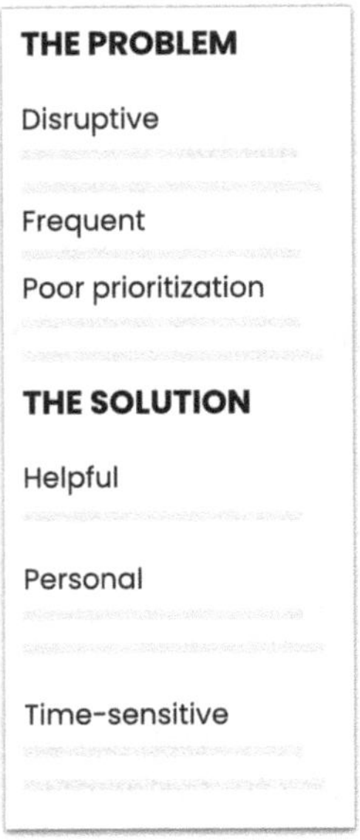

THE PROBLEM

Disruptive

Frequent

Poor prioritization

THE SOLUTION

Helpful

Personal

Time-sensitive

Figure 2-25. *Even while formatting options were very limited on a given blogging platform, I was able to use bold and various casing to break down my blog post's sections. I created hierarchy with the limited tools I had so that readers could get the general idea from reading the titles only and know exactly where to dive in further according to their interests*

Progressive Disclosure, Tell an Engaging Story

Sometimes we have a lot to tell the user, and they truly do need access to all that information. We cannot make it short enough for them to get everything they need by scanning, or even by reading quickly. In fact, if we serve it all up at once, they won't consume any of it at all. We know they won't. They'll skip on by. So we can't give it all together. But we can't take any of it away either. What's a content designer to do?

We break it up into chunks. We give it all, but small bites at a time. There is a delicate balance between giving it all, but not all at once, allowing users to consume it all comfortably, or to decide at a certain point that they don't need it anymore while still leaving the rest available to other users who do want it.

This is called progressive disclosure—a design strategy that shows users only the information they need at a given moment and hides the rest behind UI elements like accordions, tabs, or links. When done well, it reduces cognitive load and helps users focus on the task at hand. But it comes with trade-offs.

Pros include reducing overwhelm; supporting scannability; keeping designs compact where space is limited; and remaining machine-visible. With accordions specifically, search engines and LLM crawlers still "see" the full text including what's collapsed, even if humans initially see only some.

However, there is the risk of missed context. If the hierarchy isn't structured well, or if users don't notice or don't feel like expanding the accordion, they may never see important explanations, caveats, or warnings that they otherwise would have been interested in. There is also the extra interaction cost, i.e., another click, which means more friction for anyone who drills down. And there are accessibility concerns, as some implementations can be harder for screen-reader users if not properly coded.

Let's say you've considered all that, mitigated risks, and decided progressive disclosure is the right way to go. A common way to structure progressive disclosure is with an accordion element. This puts the highest level, most critical info up front and center. Users who want to drill down can do so in a single click or tap. Accordions can even have more than two layers if there are that many levels of resolution that need to be included.

An example is showing an automatic debit that will be transferred on a given date. At the highest level, all users need to be able to see is the date of the debit, the amount of the debit, how much of their revolving credit line will be available to them again after this partial repayment of loans is debited, and how many different loans are being repaid in that single debit. That's enough for most users.

Other users will want to know exactly *which* loans are being repaid in that one debit, how many payments are left on each of those loans, and some additional details, and they need to be able to get to that information easily and in close proximity to where they are. But, most users will not want to get to this level of resolution, and it's our job not to make them dizzy by putting it all in their face. Progressive disclosure via an accordion is a perfect solution here.

***Figure 2-26.** Accordions are a great way to slowly share higher and higher resolution info with users who want it, so it's digestible, without bothering at all the users who don't want or need to see it*

The same goes for security information. Everyone needs to see that an app was built with security in mind. But honestly, just the word "security" is enough for most. Let's not hold up those who are satisfied, with a bunch more details about what stands behind the claim of ensuring security. At the same time, a user looking for more meat on the topic is not going to proceed without it. Again, progressive disclosure lets you keep the highest level info out for everyone and the next level close by only for those who want it. Even in cases where everyone needs all the information, setting it up like this lets them digest a piece at a time.

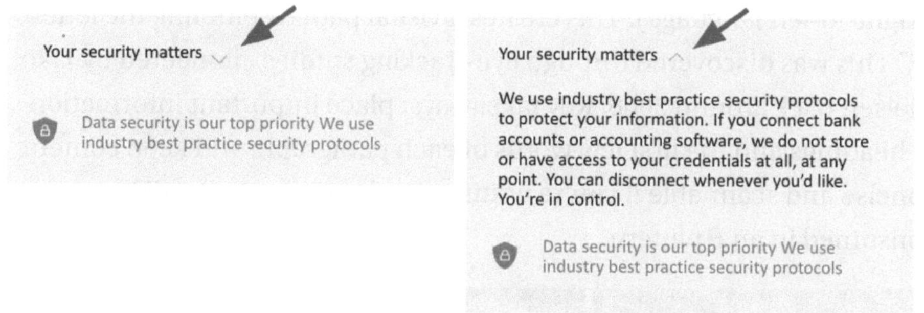

Figure 2-27. *Expand-collapse behavior lets you apply progressive disclosure in all kinds of places—even footers*

Another option is to use a link so users can decide that if they want more information, they can be taken to a pop-up or another page to get it...but make sure it's easy to come back. Be careful, for example, in a purchase flow, I wouldn't send users out to a separate browser window to read a help center page because you'll dramatically decrease the chances they come back to complete the original flow where they were gonna buy something.

Write How Users Read by Using Relevant Patterns

Understanding common reading patterns will help you design your content to match where it's most likely to be seen.

F-Pattern

The F-pattern is common on text-heavy web pages, such as articles or search results. Users first read across the top of the page, then move down slightly and read across again, but for a shorter distance. Finally, they scan down the left side of the content (flipped, of course, if we're talking about a right-to-left language). This creates a visual path resembling the letter "F." This was discovered through eye-tracking studies, pioneered by Jakob Nielsen back around 2006. Key takeaways: place important information in headings and the first few words of each paragraph, and keep content concise and scannable if you're writing an experience that will be consumed in an F pattern.

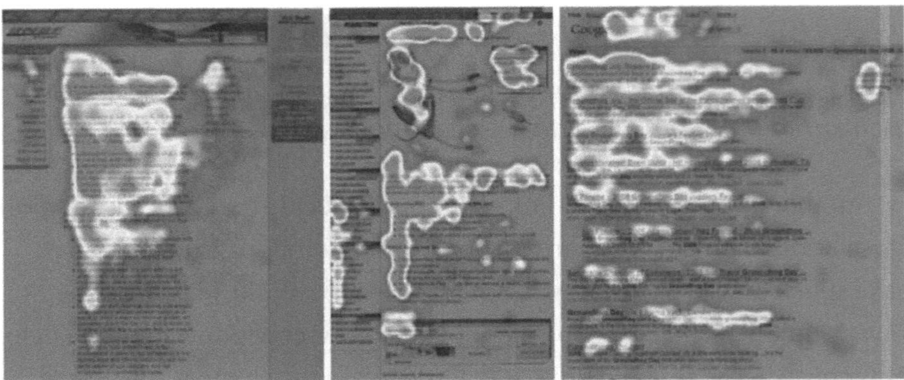

Figure 2-28. *Eye-tracking research conducted by Nielsen Norman Group, elucidated the F pattern*

Z-Pattern

The Z-pattern is typical on simpler pages with less text and more visual balance, like landing pages or homepages. Users scan from the top-left to the top-right, then diagonally down to the bottom-left, and finally across to the bottom-right—forming a "Z" shape. (Again, everything would be the other way around in a right-to-left language.) If you're writing a page likely to be read in a Z-pattern, your designer will likely put your logo top-left, place navigation or a headline across the top, and use the diagonal space for attention-grabbing visuals, or you might want to use it for key messages, and most important for the content designers, you'll end with your CTA on the bottom-right.

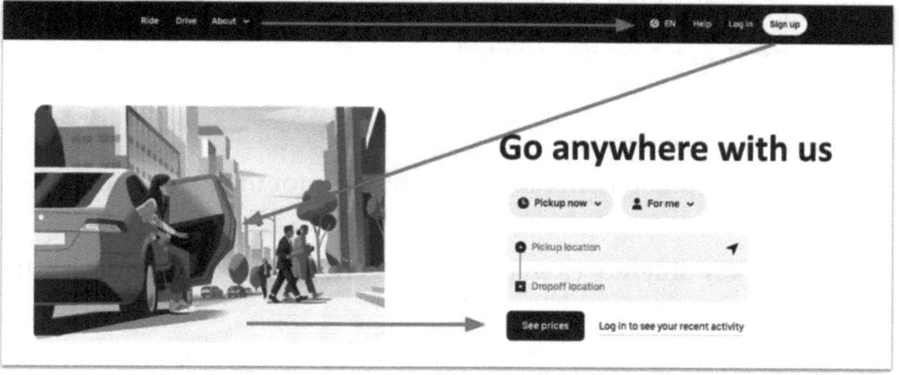

***Figure 2-29.** Knowing how the users' eyes will move across the page should guide where you write the copy so they read it in the order that you meant them to*

Ping-pong

The ping-pong pattern occurs when users' eyes bounce back and forth between focal points, like text on one side of the screen and images or media on the other. You're likely to encounter this pattern in comparison layouts like pricing tables, when users are weighing options and their eyes jump left-right-left-right to check details, and in chat interfaces or email threads, where attention moves back and forth between alternating messages.

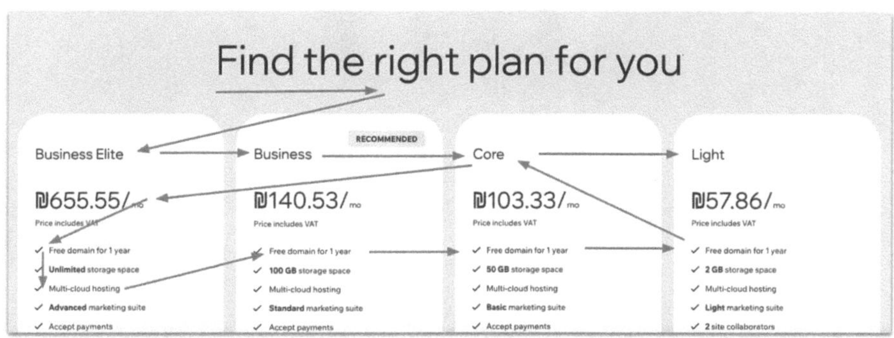

***Figure 2-30.** Pinball patterns are characteristic of price comparison experiences*

To optimize for this behavior, keep text and visuals aligned and tightly paired, so users don't get disoriented.

Use consistent spacing and design cues to help guide their attention smoothly between elements.

Keep the compared items aligned so it's easy for the eye to jump across rows.

Highlight key differences so people don't have to bounce endlessly to spot them.

Learn about common patterns at `https://www.nngroup.com/articles/how-people-read-online/`.

Lawnmower

The lawnmower pattern appears when users need to scan structured content in a grid or table—like search results, product listings, or dashboards. Eyes move across a row from side to side, then drop down to the next row and scan back the other way—just like a lawnmower going back and forth across a lawn.

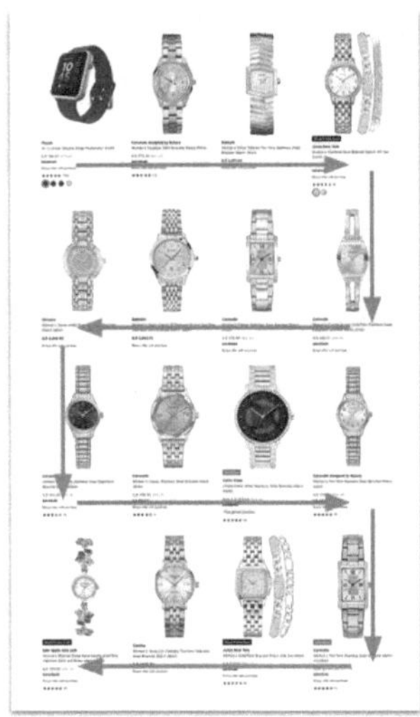

Figure 2-31. *Lawnmower patterns are characteristic of product listings on ecommerce sites*

To support this pattern, make sure rows are evenly spaced, use clear labels and columns, and avoid clutter that might interrupt the horizontal flow.

Bottom line: Don't try to change the way the eyes are jumping—take that as a given and smooth out the experience around that starting point. As always, understand where the users already are and meet them there.

Avoid Ampersands

Ampersands are a symbol that means the word "and." It started out as a combination of two letters—et—which means "and" in Latin. While there was a period hundreds of years ago when it was mainstream and even considered a 27th letter of the alphabet, these days it's more stylish than meaningful.

Because it has fallen out of mainstream use, I wouldn't call it "plain English" anymore, and we know how important it is in UX writing to use plain English as much as possible. While using ampersands might make you feel fancy when writing them, they narrow the audience who will know what you mean. Ampersands are not inclusive for people with a low literacy level, people whose first language isn't English, and people below a certain age who hardly interact with handwritten text or decorative typefaces and are mostly exposed to digital texts where "and" is generally written out. Ampersands are also not accessible—screen readers may read out "ampersand" instead of "and," disrupting the experience for people who rely on a screen reader. When weighing the pros and cons of using ampersands in your microcopy, you'll see they're rarely justified.

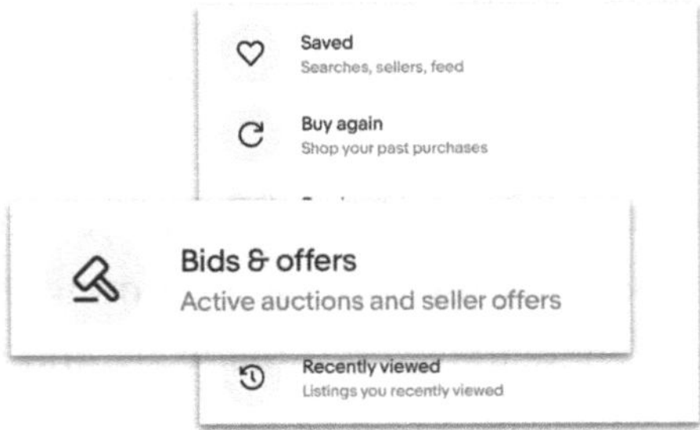

Figure 2-32. *Stylized fonts can confound the difficulty in understanding ampersands*

Adjust Hierarchy If Copy Repeats Itself

If you find yourself repeating yourself (again and again), chances are you're using copy that belongs at a different place in the content hierarchy. For example, if you have a few menu items that all end with "request", like "Re-open request", "Cancel request", and "Delete request", the word "request" should be written only once, at a higher level in the hierarchy, which makes it apply to all of the menu items without being repeated in each menu option. Similarly, if you have "shop" on a primary, secondary, and tertiary CTA all in a row, I'd recommend pulling out "shop" altogether and putting it higher up, like in the language before the interaction.

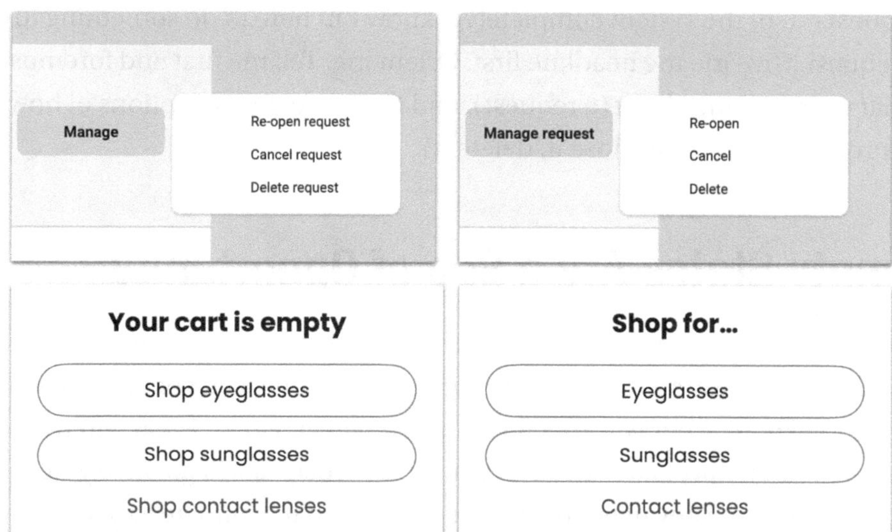

Figure 2-33. *If you find yourself repeating yourself again and again, chances are you're using copy that belongs higher up in the hierarchy. In the examples above, we can push back "request" and push up "Shop"*

First of all, why would we require the user to read the same word again and again when we can save them time and cognitive load and let them read it just once? Second, repeating the frontloaded word really hurts scannability. The user has to scoot their eyes past the word that repeats itself to understand the menu option...on every single row. In fact, Neilson Norman Group found that there's a "bypassing reading pattern" in eye-tracking studies, where users deliberately skip the first words of the line when multiple lines of text in a list start the same way (`https://www.nngroup.com/articles/f-shaped-pattern-reading-web-content/`).

This is not only true for when the repeated word is frontloaded, but also when it appears anywhere string after string.

If I click once on "Manage request," I know that all of the choices I'll be given are to do with my request. Whether I want to re-open a request I've previously closed, cancel a request I no longer want processed, or delete a request out of the system completely, I know I'm here to do something to a request. Give me the headline first. Orient me. Tell me first and foremost what we're talking about (a request), and then give me my options of how to proceed (re-open it, close it, delete it).

Empty States Are a Sea of Opportunity

Empty states are the screens a user sees when there is no data or content to display. For example, you are using an app that lets you collect recipes into a cookbook—but you haven't chosen any recipes yet. What you'll see instead is an empty state: a screen where your recipes will go once you've collected some. They need to go somewhere, and it would be awkward if the place where they go only appeared after you'd found recipes, so that space exists at the beginning, but empty.

As UXers, we try to avoid surprising users. We want to manage expectations for seamless experiences that feel smooth and not startling. So what we'll do is create a space for recipes, even though you haven't collected any yet, so that you know where they will show up eventually—but we can't leave that space blank. First of all, blank spaces tend to look like bugs. Imagine you open an app and get a big ol' screen of nothing. You'll definitely think it's broken. As content designers, we follow a few best practices to make the most of empty state spaces.

Figure 2-34. *Dropbox has some inspiring empty states*

Confirm the Void Is There On Purpose

The first best practice is to explain why the empty state is empty and to confirm that it's empty on purpose. What is that space being reserved for? If you tell me this is a place for recipes but I haven't collected any yet, now I understand why the empty state is empty. I understand that it's not blank because it's broken but rather it's blank intentionally as a placeholder for me when I'm ready. Now I'm oriented and feel good that I know what's going on.

Motivate Users to Fill the Void with Goodness

Next, let the user know how to fill it! Working off the assumption that space is being reserved for something valuable—like the recipes I'll be collecting into a cookbook—you have to let the user know how to achieve that goal. If you're saving the space for recipes, how do I collect them? Do I start with a search bar? Do I peruse a different tab? Do I send telepathic vibes out into the universe and then recipes appear in a swirl of fairy dust? Anything is possible. As the user, I have no idea.

So I've encountered an empty space, and you explain why it's empty. Next, explain how to fill it. This is also the place to communicate why they should *want* to fill it. In my experience, filling empty states is usually directly tied to the product's success metrics. Most likely, it is in the company's and the user's best interest to fill the empty state, so add to the "how" a healthy dose of "why." What's in it for the user? What's the value proposition of this flow and space?

Facilitate Action

The third best practice for empty space content design is to let the user actually take action toward filling it. In other words, it's not good enough to describe how to fill the empty state: "Search popular recipes and tap your favorites"—leave the user a button that takes them directly to search functionality!

In short, empty state best practices are to explain why it's empty, explain how to fill it, and give them the means to fill it right there and then.

If adding elements, like a button that was not in the original design—not just writing words on existing elements—sounds like more than you realized was in our purview, then it's time to talk about microcopy vs. content design. Microcopy is indeed the little bits of text all over the experience, and writing them is a big part of what content design practitioners do. However, it's far from the only thing we do. Our mandate is to guide users with content, and that can mean not only deciding how the content reads but also where it's placed on the page, if it's placed on the page. For example, think about the ping pong and lawnmower patterns we talked about earlier. It's a content design best practice to put the words in the order the user will read them, not just write the words themselves, even if a designer's original wireframe has the words in different places.

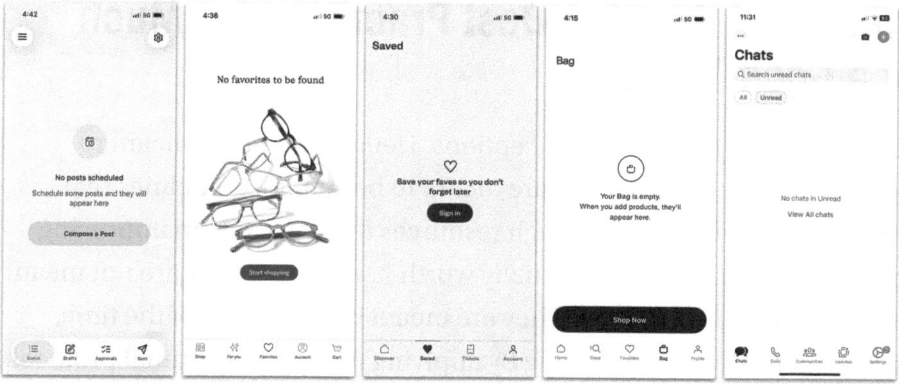

Figure 2-35. *All of these empty states confirm that the void is there on purpose—simply by not being completely blank and explaining what would go here if it existed, they check that box. The third is the only one that really tries to motivate users: "...so you don't forget later." It's the only one that really gives a reason for why I should care about filling the empty space, as opposed to simply describing how to. All but the last one facilitate action by offering a button. The last one doesn't facilitate action because there is no action to be taken. At the same time, it doesn't want to leave the user at a dead end, so it provides an interaction to pave a way forward for the user*

Breaking Best Practices

We said that best practices are super helpful heuristics for writing product copy. They serve as shortcuts that save time and money and are a way for the content design community to codify insights in a way that serves more users of more apps—we share our wisdom to learn from each other's experiences and user research. Sounds like a dream! So why would we want to break best practices? Because believe you me, there is a time and a place.

When and Why Are Best Practices Too Much of a Good Thing?

First of all, every rule has its exceptions. Heuristics are not meant to replace critical thinking; they are meant to be general guidelines that usually work and save us enough resources that investing in improving them in a specific case isn't usually worth it. However, they are not meant to be fail-safes or catch-alls. They are meant to work most of the time, enough of the time that starting by applying them is the optimal protocol. But starting with them doesn't mean ending with them.

There will be cases where you start writing copy according to a best practice and then take a step back and realize that you've hit a case where it's not worth it, where the outcome is not good enough. If our rules never had exceptions, it wouldn't mean they're good rules; it would mean that we're not thinking critically or realistically enough because the world is one hell of a complicated place. If we think long and hard enough, we'll find the exception to every rule of thumb. How do we know when it is indeed time to break the rules?

The underlying assumptions do not apply: First of all, if an underlying assumption of the best practice is not accurate, we can assume that, in this case, the best practice is not valid. For example, the underlying assumption of applying "scannable" to our copy is that we want to move users through flows quickly and effortlessly. If we are writing for a flow where we want users to move slowly and carefully, like signing a mortgage, "scannable" as a general approach probably does not apply. It's time to break the best practice and use words that will force users to slow down and read every letter—not glance and click.

Or take, for example, abbreviations that have become more conventional than the spelled-out version, like "Q&A." In these cases, I would break the best practice of avoiding ampersands because that best practice is based on the assumption that ampersands are not a symbol that is universally understood; however, in unique cases like "Q&A," it is probably *more* well recognized and easy to consume than "questions and answers" or, even worse, "Q and A."

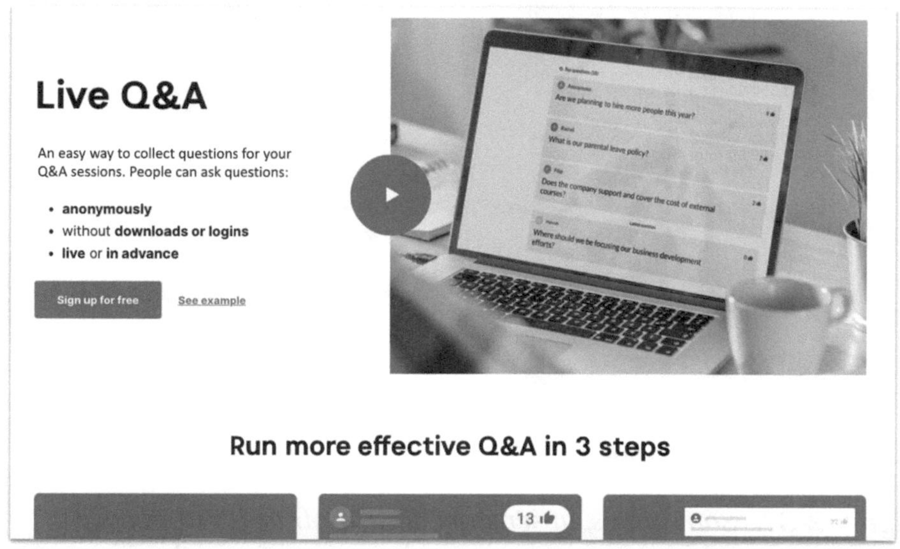

Figure 2-36. *Sometimes one best practice will trump another, like in Q&A, where convention trumps ampersand guidelines*

The best practice does not serve our users: Another exception would be if the outcome of following a best practice does not best serve our users. Let's use "scannable" in a mortgage signing flow again. Making it easy for them to read quickly and superficially is not what serves them best in this case. We need to break the best practice in order to protect our users' best interests.

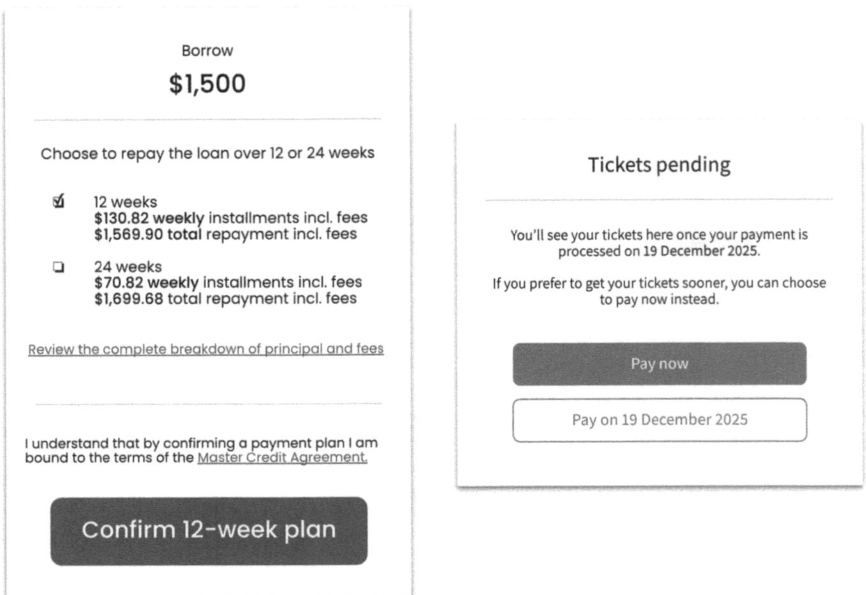

Figure 2-37. *Sometimes, at sensitive touchpoints, it's in the user's best interest to slow down. We need to help them for both of our sakes*

The best practice does not serve our product: Similarly, we know it's time to break a best practice if the outcome does not best serve our business.

For example, if there is an action that we need to allow users to take, but taking it will cost our business money, we might not use an "actionable CTA." We might choose a less motivating structure, while the product flow, functionality, and behavioral UX remain unchanged. We might write "Payment options" instead of "Repay early" if we want users to be able to repay early and save on fees at the expense of the business, but not actively encourage them to do so.

Another example is when I was writing a genetic survey product. This was not the time to be concise. First of all, we're talking about collecting sensitive information, and users want all the details. They have questions and need the answers up front in order to engage. This is not the time to be quick and rush them through. Even users who don't plan to read long copy still want to see the long copy there. In an area like this, simply having a critical mass of content feels trustworthy, serious, reliable. Optimally introducing a product in this case required breaking the best practice of "concise." Less concise was better for users who wanted to feel more secure and better for the product because now more users would answer the surveys.

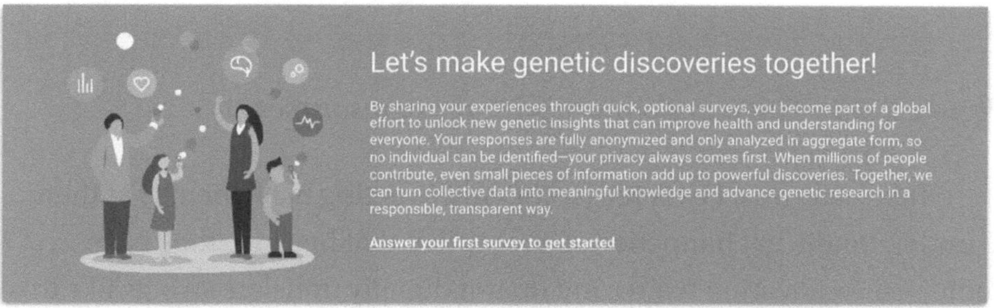

Figure 2-38. *Sometimes simply having a critical mass of content feels trustworthy, serious, reliable. In those cases, you'll also have a small but important group of users who want to read it all*

The best practice puts the copy at (significant) odds with the product voice: Lastly, I'd break a best practice if the outcome is at significant odds with the product voice. For example, while we generally would avoid slang, if we are writing for a niche market of users who expect us to speak their language, and would not see us as credible if we weren't tuned in to the language they use with each other including slang, it's time to break the best practice and stick with the personality our users know and love.

Slack is one of the products most well known for its voice, and they leaned into it in a validation error when creating a private channel with a name that is too long. "Blerg, that's a bit too long!"

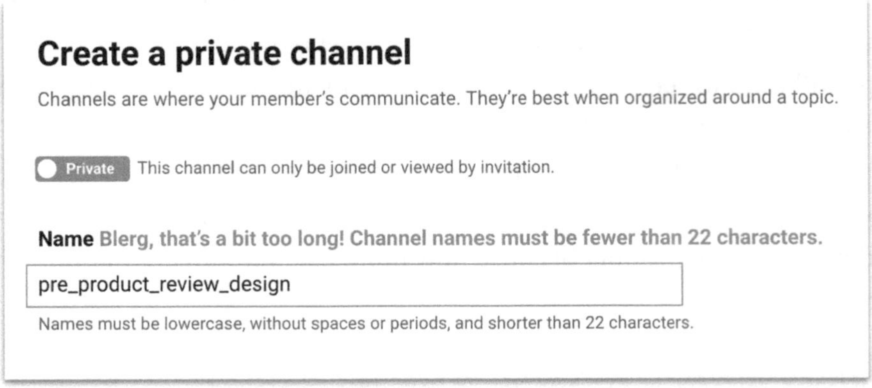

Create a private channel

Channels are where your member's communicate. They're best when organized around a topic.

Private This channel can only be joined or viewed by invitation.

Name Blerg, that's a bit too long! Channel names must be fewer than 22 characters.

pre_product_review_design

Names must be lowercase, without spaces or periods, and shorter than 22 characters.

Figure 2-39. *You can do more with more resources*

When I saw this, I tweeted (it was still tweeting back then...) at them to understand what happened. They replied that because they have dedicated localization teams and do not directly translate strings like this one, from language to language, they give themselves more wiggle room within each language. That felt fair. See their full explanation on their blog: `https://slack.com/blog/collaboration/how-we-localize-slack`.

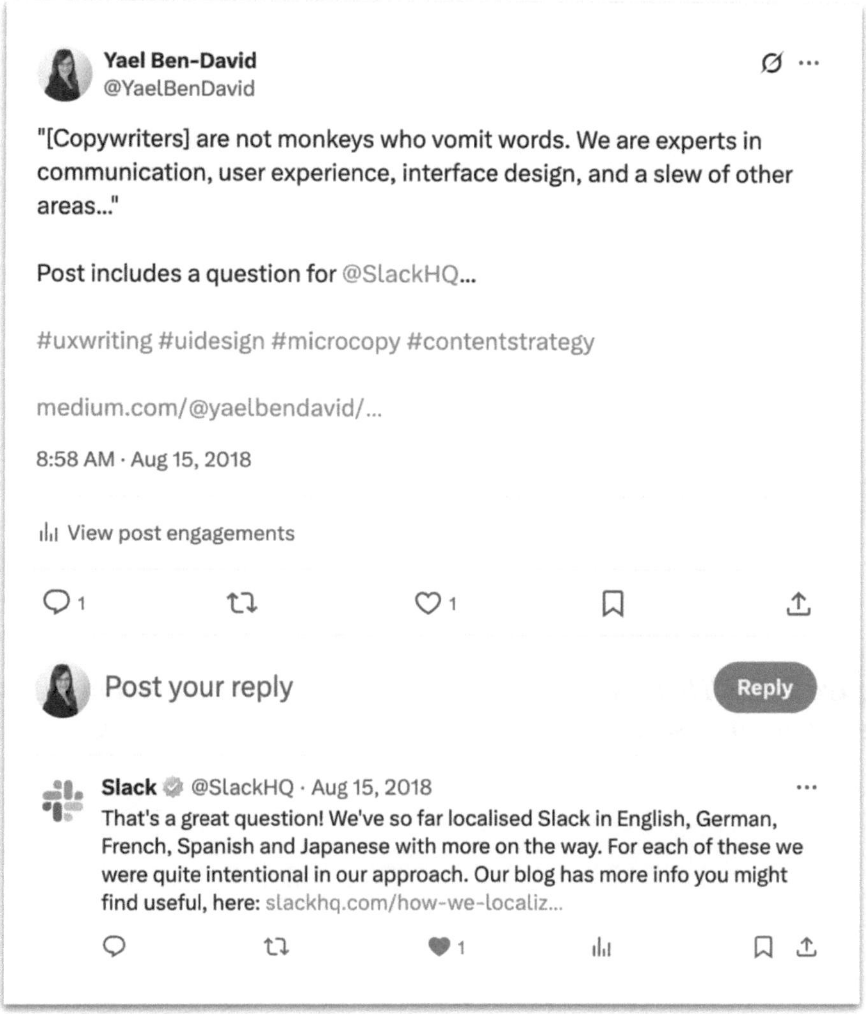

Figure 2-40. *When you ask, you learn!*

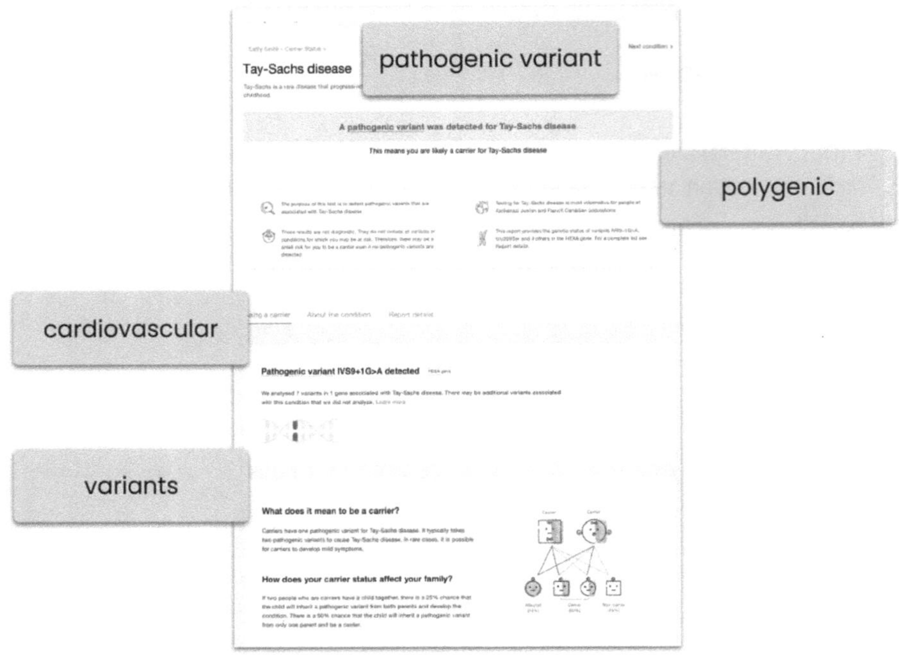

Figure 2-41. *There is a middle ground with jargon—if you need to use it, you can use it in addition to, not instead of, plain language*

CHAPTER 3

Voice and Tone

I often hear "voice and tone" as if it's one word, or even worse, "tone of voice." Voice and tone are two distinct things, both critical to get right. Let's start with voice and then move on to tone and how to use them both at once.

Voice Is Personality

When my parents read my writing, they say it's as if I'm sitting next to them speaking. Even as they read silently in their heads 7,000 miles away, they can hear me talking, hear my voice. If our users see copy out of context and immediately visualize our brand and feel our product is close because they "hear our voice", that relationship is deep. Those users are less likely to churn and more likely to recommend the product in their circles.

Voice is the personality of your product. If your product were a person, how would you describe their personality? What is your immediate impression of them when you meet for a first drink? How would you describe them after getting to know them better over time? Are they fun or serious? Are they philosophical or grounded, more interested in the concrete here and now than thought experiments and dreams? The words you use to describe your product voice are words you'd use to describe a human you know (or wish you knew).

Y. Ben-David, *The Fundamentals of UX Writing*, Apress Pocket Guides,
https://doi.org/10.1007/979-8-8688-2350-3_3

Voice Manifests in Content and Character

It's both **what** a person chooses to speak about as well as **how** they sound that makes up a personality. For example, I may have two friends who are both really intense, but one is a stay-at-home mom constantly researching child development and measuring her kid, while the other is a single-by-choice person who attends all the engineering-related conferences around the world and codes in all their free time. Those sound like different people. I might describe both as "intense," but spending time conversing with them does not feel the same.

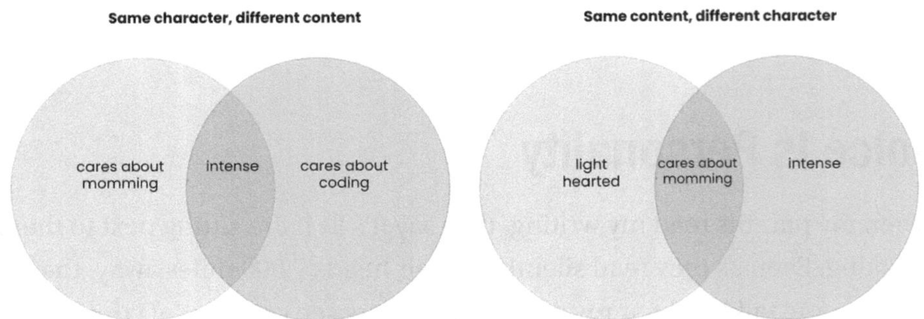

Figure 3-1. *It's both what the person chooses to speak about as well as how they sound that make up a personality. You need both when defining your product voice*

I also may have a third friend who also loves coding conferences and spends all her free time blogging about the latest tech…but her blog is full of lighthearted puns, and at every conference, she posts duck face selfies.

The first two friends share character (intense) but not content; the last two share content (coding) but not character. All three each have a unique personality (voice), which is a combination of their individual character and content. You need to decide the voice of your product and express it in content and character. What do you talk about and how?

Voice Should Be Consistent

Your voice should not change throughout the product experience. It should also be in sync with the marketing brand voice. Otherwise, marketing is like a profile in a dating app, which ends up communicating something very different than what the first in-person date is actually like. Yuck. Pick a voice, describe your personality. Express it through your choices of what to write about and how. Stick with it.

There is an exception. People do change. They shouldn't change from interaction to interaction—that would be weird, and you would likely trust them less, be less comfortable around them, and spend less time together. Not a position that we want our product to put our users in. But people can change once or twice-ish over a lifetime. Say, after a traumatic event or a mind-blowing epiphany on a retreat in the wilderness. They may come back a changed person, talking about different things and speaking in a different way. That's OK, and that happens in product voice too. It's called a rebrand.

I worked for a company where we decided to shift upmarket. We wanted to switch from a voice that resonated with the persona of a struggling small-time entrepreneur with whom we spoke about getting financing to make payroll (content) in an empathetic way (character) to a voice that resonated with the persona of a successful entrepreneur with a bright future. We started to speak about getting financing to invest in new marketing campaigns (content) in a forward-looking way (character). For example: "Invest in growth" replaced "Never miss payroll again." The new voice talked about success with enthusiasm, while the old voice talked about shortcomings with a sense of relief. But once we made the shift, we stayed consistent for a very long time.

Voice Needs to Resonate with *Your* Audience, Not *Every* Audience

In *The Man Who Lied to His Laptop*, Clifford Nass talks about how language is uniquely human, and therefore, we automatically expect interactions using language to feel human, even if the interaction is actually with a machine. Some humans we like, others we don't. Some of the humans whom I like, you don't, and vice versa. That's OK. And products are the same way.

When we choose a product voice, we choose, in part, based on who it is we hope to resonate with. I want to use the content and character that will connect with my audience, even if it won't connect with someone else's audience. Focus on your audience, not the whole world. We all know that people-pleasing person who tries to win over everyone. It doesn't tend to work out. Better to hone in on the users your product is for and be the personality that connects with them at the expense of those your product is not for. A quality fit over quantity relationship is more likely to lead to long-term success.

I hope all of that has got you thinking deeply about your product voice, but thinking is not enough. You gotta get it down on paper (screen). Once codified, you can reference it in the future for the sake of staying consistent yourself; share it with other team members for them to align to; and use it as a baseline to springboard from as your product evolves over time. You need a voice guide.

How to Create a Voice Guide

A voice guide has three parts:

- "We are..."
- "We are not..."
- Examples of getting it right and getting it wrong

Step 1: We Are...

"We are..." is a list of characteristics that describe your personality. Your product voice may be friendly, genuine, and relaxed. Or you may be better described as technical, expert, and direct. There are definitely products out there with each of these voices.

Choosing the right voice depends on what's appropriate for your product space and goals and what resonates with your user base. Let's take a security app that I've installed in order to protect my privacy online. The app space and goals are intense; the personality should be alert, hyper-focused, and up to date on the latest developments in cybersecurity. That's who I'm looking to interact with in this experience, that's the voice that will resonate with me, instill trustworthiness, and foster a long-term relationship. It reflects the app space and goals and what I'm expecting and looking for in this context. It will be expressed in the content and character of the copy throughout the product experience.

However, I expect to interact with someone totally different offline, after hours, when I'm looking to put my feet up at the end of the day, watch a good show, and order takeout. If my entertainment apps feel intense, I'm outta there. I don't want to interact with Mr. Cybersecurity right now—I'm looking to hang out with someone chill, not in a rush or hyper-focused. So take a minute (or several days or weeks in collaboration with others) thinking through who you are. Are you the security app or are you entertainment? What's the right content and character for the relationship? Make a list of those traits. It might look something like this.

Exercise for Starting Your Voice Guide: We Are…

We are...	...but we are not

We are...	...but we are not
Confident, knowledgeable	
Direct	
Supportive	
Positive, focused on the future	

Figure 3-2. *Start your voice guide with a list of character traits that describe the personality of your product*

Step 2: We Are Not…

You just described a personality. I'm going to imagine a person who fits your description and act it out. Now I'm going to ask three other writers to do the same thing. How similar do you think our performances will be? Not similar enough.

We are all going to have a slightly different interpretation of what those character traits sound like, and so we need a little more guidance. You have just described the bull's eye of the target—you've described the ideal voice. But if we miss a little, what might that sound like? What guardrails can you give us to get us back on track so that we all align?

Previously, we set up a voice guide and started filling in the first part, "We are…." One of our "We are…" traits was "direct." Now, imagine a bunch of writers are writing copy that is direct. Where might they miss a little? Might it come out dry? "We are not…" should be something you might hit if you miss the bull's eye of "We are…."

Trap #1

"We are not…" is **not the opposite** of "We are…." Any writer worth their salt who is aiming for "direct" should not write in a way that is "indirect." If they need your voice guide to know that, they have bigger problems. "We are not…" opposites of "We are…" are not valuable. It's easy when writing a voice guide to list opposites in the first two columns, so I'm highlighting this as trap #1. Don't fall into it. If the "We are not…" column becomes a thesaurus of antonyms, you've missed a critical opportunity to raise the value and efficacy of your voice guide. When "We are not…" is used right, it levels up all the copy in your product.

Trap #2

There are certain characteristics **no product** wants to be, like rude, mean, arrogant, vague (ok, ok, I'm sure there's an exception out there, but go with me on this). Again, this is something a writer shouldn't need your voice guide for, in order to avoid. Calling these traits out in your "...we are not" is not valuable either. "We are not..." should be something that some product out there would want to be, just not yours.

Trap #3

The whole point of "We are not..." is to serve as a guardrail, or an upper and lower limit, for different writers with different interpretations of the list of personality traits under "We are...".

The only way "We are not..." is helpful is if it's close enough to the target that a writer actually might hit it by accident, notice it's in the guide, and use that as a flag to get back on track. Don't write "We are nots..." that are irrelevant in the copy process.

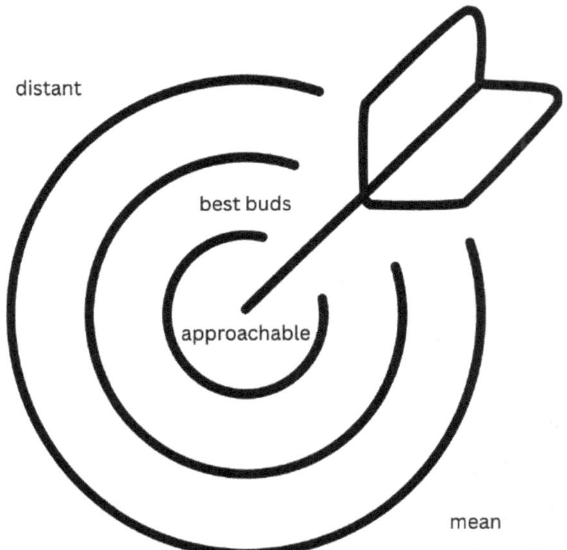

Figure 3-3. *If you are aiming for the "We are" personality trait of "Approachable," a writer might accidentally write copy that feels like "Best buds," so "Best buds" is a valuable "We are not." Trap #3 dodged!*

The opposite of Approachable is Distant, so using Distant as a "We are not" lands you squarely in Trap #1.

Also, no app wants to be Mean, so using Mean as a guideline is pretty useless. Mean means you fell for Trap #2.

Exercise for Continuing Your Voice Guide: We Are Not…

Go back to the last exercise where you set up your voice guide and filled out "We are…". Now add the column "We are not…". Carefully check that each "We are not…" does not fall into any of the three common traps. This may take several iterations and some hairpulling gout, but what doesn't kill you makes you stronger, and this is gonna make your copy strategy going forward a beast. Coffee and company recommended tools for this exercise.

We are...	...but we are not
Confident, knowledgeable	**All knowing.** We are aware users are coming to us for information but they are not looking for us to make decisions for them, like perhaps a financial investment advisory app would.
Direct	**Dry.** We "say it like it is" but not as distantly as a fancy bank might. We still have some color and lightness, but without compromising clarity.
Supportive	**Assuming.** We reach out to our users and support them through the experience without assuming that we know exactly what they're going through because everybody's journey is different.
Positive, focused on the future	**Dreamers.** We talk about potential but always ground the vision to practical next steps. It's not a creative writing app or interested in abstract inspiration.

Figure 3-4. *The beginning of your voice guide after Step 1, "We are," and Step 2, "We are not."*

Step 3: Examples Are What Make Your Guide Come to Life

"We are" is your bull's eye, and "we are not" is the next ring in the target—it's where you end up if you miss a little bit, which is why you need that guardrail to get you back on track. But what does landing darts actually look like? An example is worth a million guidelines.

Keeping it all high level and theoretical might work for a team of a single expert at a specific point in time, but when you're trying to align across stakeholders, teams, or even yourself over time, examples are massively helpful. Showing, not just telling, helps it all sink in and take your voice guide from an academic exercise to a practical, applicable tool.

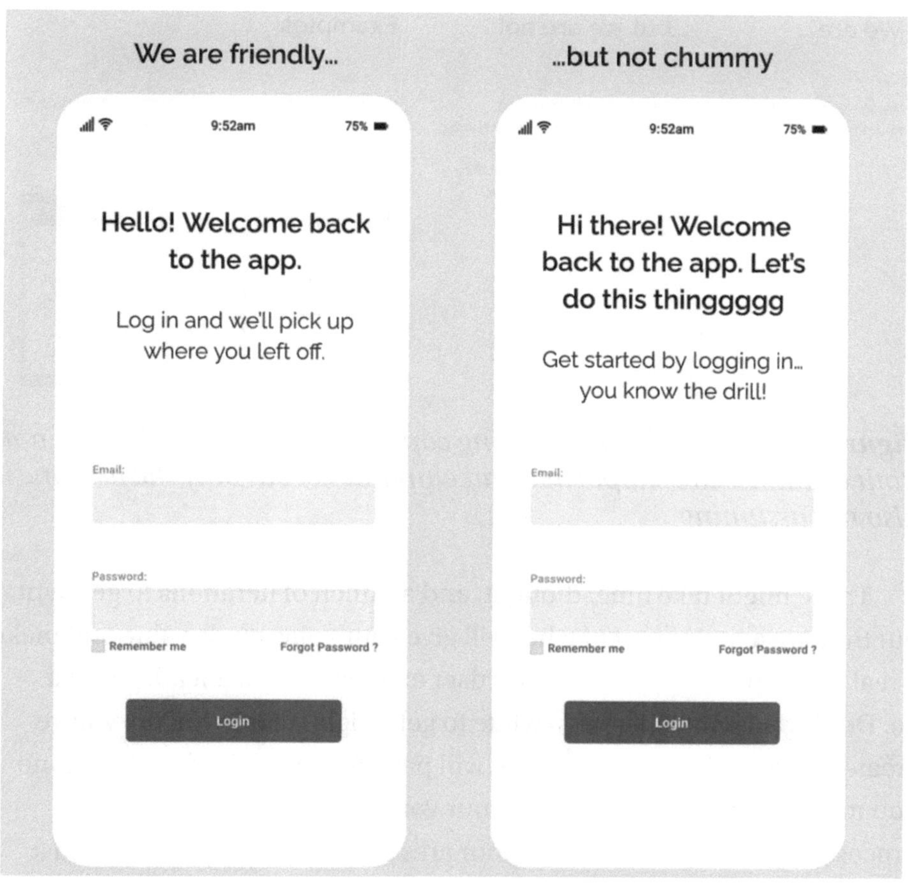

Figure 3-5. *Example of adjusting copy for "we are" and "we are not." Here, both iterations indeed align to "we are friendly"; only the first iteration* ***also*** *aligns to "we are not chummy". The second iteratoin is an example of getting it wrong*

It's critical to show examples of getting it right and examples of getting it wrong. Distinguishing between the two is where the value is. That's where the ah-ha moment lives. And who doesn't love a good old ah-ha moment.

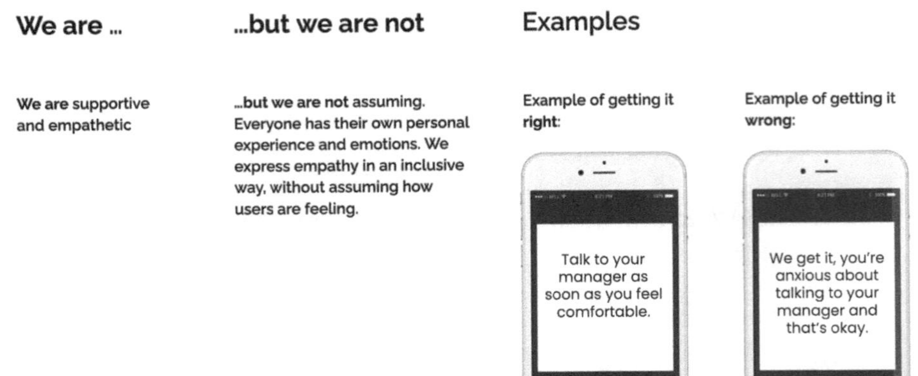

Figure 3-6. *Examples of adjusting copy for "we are" and "we are not." Both examples are supportive and empathetic, but only the first one is also not assuming*

These might take time, thought, and a bunch of iterations to get right, but they are a major part of what will give your voice guide value and make a real downstream impact on your user experience. Go ahead, give it a go. Don't give it up if it takes a while to get it right—once you do, you've created an asset for your team that will pay off many-fold, for a long time. You may want to include users of your voice guide in this part of the process to get early feedback on your ares and are nots. Sit together in a room, and you may see yourself as everyone works, where your original guidelines still need some touching up, based on how users of the guide interact with them while trying to write copy for the examples column.

We are...	We are not...	✓ Good example	✗ Bad example
In touch, read the room	Assuming	You're eligible for up to $7,000	Congrats! You're eligible for up to $7,000
In it together, on your side	Overly sympathetic.	The information you're looking for is not here but perhaps we can help at help@help.com	Sorry the page doesn't exist. We'll do our best to help—contact help@help.com.

Figure 3-7. *Example of the beginning of a voice guide for a financial product with a wide audience. They want to show that they are in touch with the customer, but not overly so in a way that feels assuming. For example, they shouldn't assume that when a user is approved for a $7,000 loan, that's good news—what if a particular user was hoping for $20k? Similarly, being on the user's side can be a differentiator from banks who might make users feel like they are always looking to take advantage of them, but being overly sympathetic feels unprofessional and weird. For example, if info is missing from the site, the product should focus on helping the user get what they need somewhere else, not getting hung up on a silly technical glitch that might not be their fault and that getting sentimental over won't help anyone*

We are...	We are not...	✓ Good example	✗ Bad example
Supportive, empathetic	Assuming	Talk to your manager about your leave as soon as you feel comfortable.	It's perfectly normal to have some anxiety about talking to your manager about your leave.
Direct	Dry, unemotional	Wondering what happens to your benefits while on leave? We've got answers.	Here's what happens to your benefits while you're on leave.

Figure 3-8. *Example of the beginning of a voice guide for a product employees use to manage extended absences from work. Again, it's important for this supportive app not to sound assuming—some users might have anxiety about talking to their managers, but others might not, and we don't want to accidentally make them feel like they should with our copy! Additionally, leave takers have a lot of info to process, so it's important to be direct, but that doesn't mean they don't want to feel like a human being is holding their hand. It's a fine line to walk, but a good writer can do it. I believe in you!*

Tone Maps Because Context Matters

While voice stays consistent (see exception in previous chapter), tone adjusts to the current context. Voice is the personality; tone is how the personality manifests in different scenarios.

Tone Is a Spectrum

At the point when our doctor is talking with her patient about the harsh side effects of treatment, her tone will likely become even more serious than when she first welcomed the patient in the front door because "serious" and "lighthearted" are not binary; there is a gradient that she slides along.

This will manifest in your tone documentation—your tone maps—as each touchpoint is plotted with different magnitudes. You won't just plot touchpoints "above the line" (lighthearted, in our case) or "below the line" (serious, in our case). They will be a little above or a lot above, or a little below or a lot below the line, to represent the **direction** and **intensity** of the tone in the moment.

For the sake of our example tone map, let's assume we're talking about a medical app instead of an actual doctor. At the beginning of the diagnosis flow, the user gets confirmation of a serious diagnosis that was previously communicated in person by her doctor. Then, she can review the treatment plan and the side effects. At the end of the flow, as part of the next steps, she is reminded of the comforting benefits available in the app as she goes through treatment.

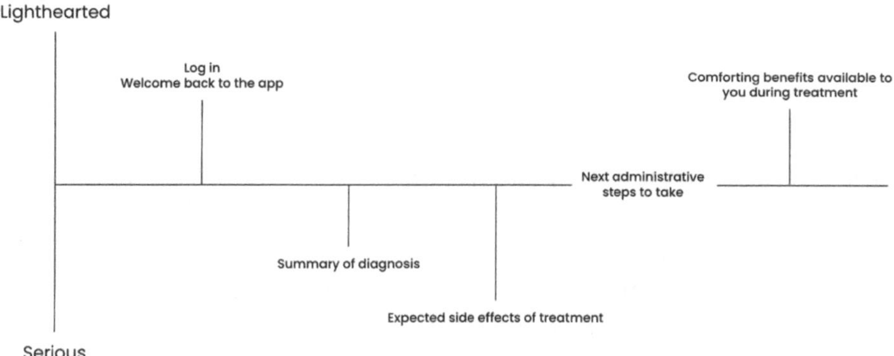

***Figure 3-9.** You can prepare tone maps for certain flows or for an entire user lifecycle from onboarding to churn to resurrection and beyond*

Notice that as the user moves through the flow, from screen to screen, touch point to touch point (left to right on the tone map), the tone changes from lighthearted to serious to more serious to neutral and back to lighthearted. This still feels a bit theoretical, so let's think about how the actual copy might sound.

Start with the first touch point on the map above, the login screen. On our map, this copy should have a lighthearted tone. It might say, "Welcome back. Glad to see you again!" If our copy does not align with our tone map and is written in a serious tone instead, it might say, "Log in. Log in to view your medical data." Both versions communicate the same message: You're logging into the app and not for the first time. But which feels like the more natural, comfortable interaction?

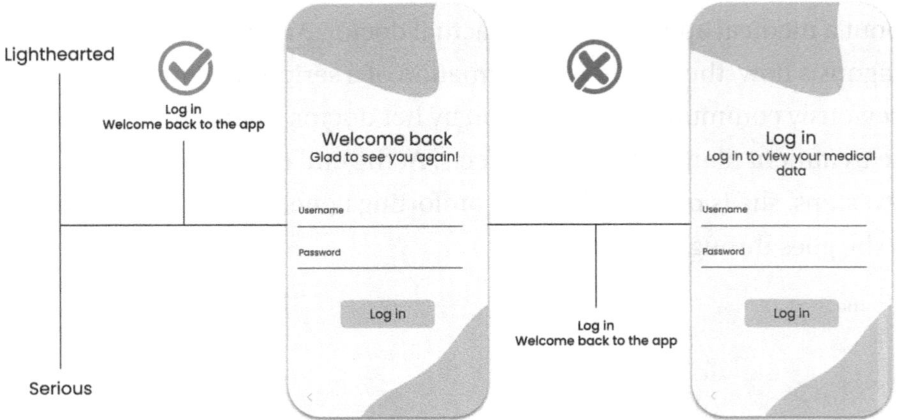

Figure 3-10. *In tone maps, like in voice guides and other educational materials, examples are gold. Good examples are the difference between users of your guidelines enjoying Eureka moments and applying your guidelines correctly vs. your guidelines getting stale on a shelf because no one's interested*

Let's repeat the exercise with the next touchpoint on the tone map: Summary of diagnosis. In this context, it's appropriate for the tone to be serious, below the line. Titles and labels might read, "Summary of diagnosis, Diagnosis, Diagnosis in layman's terms, Test results, and Diagnosed by." I would certainly not want this copy written above the line, in a lighthearted tone! That would come off as confusing at best and insensitive and unprofessional at worst.

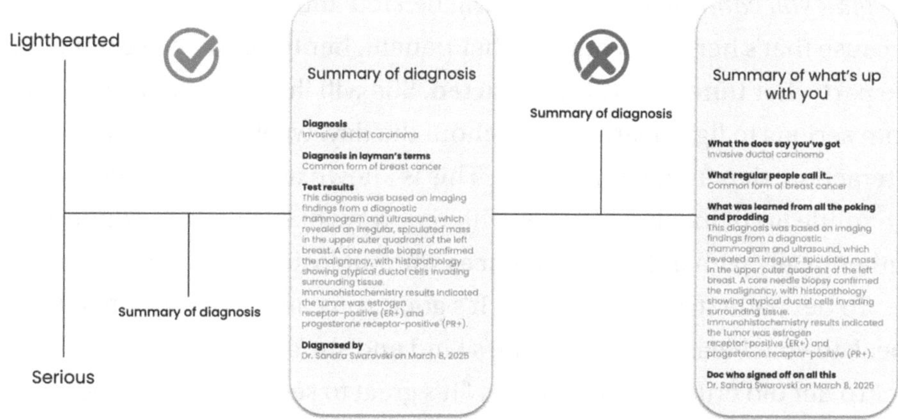

Figure 3-11. *Remember when including examples that examples of a guideline followed incorrectly can be even more informative than examples of guidelines implemented well*

Balancing Voice and Tone

Take a young doctor who is a kind, warm, gentle person. She's soft spoken and assumes good intent when talking to her patients. That's her personality, that's who she is. That's her voice. Maybe one day, she'll go through something traumatic that will make her hard and cold and look for the worst in people (i.e., voice change). But for now, people who know her describe her as kind, warm, and positive. That's who she is, and that doesn't change throughout the day or year.

Now imagine she's breaking bad news to a patient. She sounds different than when she's making small talk at her grandparents' 50th wedding anniversary, a glass or three of champagne in, spotting her high school crush across the room. Her voice—her personality—stays the same, but her tone adjusts in different contexts.

Voice can hold steady, and tone can adjust even when the actual content of the communication is the same. For example, she might want to communicate the exact same message to her patient and her old crush:

I'm glad you came here today. She will be kind and warm in both scenarios because that's her voice, but with her patient, her **tone** will be **serious;** at the party, her **tone** will be **lighthearted**. She will fluctuate on the spectrum from serious to lighthearted throughout the day, week, interaction to interaction, depending on context. This is known as code-switching—the subtle art of moving between different ways of speaking to connect authentically with different audiences without losing one's core voice.

To her patient, she might say, "It's good you came in today. I need to speak to you. Please sit down." She's kind and she's serious.

To her old crush, she might say, "It's great to see you! How wonderful that you came today. Let's get a drink and catch up." She's warm and lighthearted.

It's critical to get tone right: Imagine how unsettling it would be if the doctor delivered a poor prognosis in a lighthearted tone or how awkward it would be if, with a long face, she greeted an old pal at a party. It would be unsettling emotionally and confusing cognitively. It would not be an optimal interaction, and it's not the experience we want to create for our users.

Casual vs. Conversational Because They Are Absolutely Not the Same Thing

The difference between "conversational" and "casual" is not well understood by most stakeholders, and as content designers, we get pushback to conversational copy because "it's too casual." That's like saying a party is too lively—parties should always be lively, maybe you mean too loud? But lively and loud are not the same thing. You can have lively without loud, and you can have loud without lively, and you can have both together, and you can have a party that is neither. So it is with conversational and casual.

Conversational

"Conversational" simply means writing how a human would talk and not like a computer. For example, that might mean using positive contractions, e.g., I'll, we're. (Avoiding negative contractions is a best practice because users tend to scan copy quickly and miss the "not" in "do not," for example, when it's written as "don't," and more often than not, the "not" is critical. There is less at stake with positive contractions, which is why they do not need to be avoided in the same way. The exception to avoiding negative contractions would be in very light situations where the message does not have a lot of gravity. For example, I would write, "You are not approved for a mortgage," not "aren't approved for a mortgage," because that's heavy, but I'd be OK with "Not your jam? Don't worry" because that's not an important sentence anyway.

However, "conversational" is not a free-for-all. For example, it's usually still best to avoid slang for the sake of inclusivity and translations. "Conversational" doesn't mean write how your 12-year-old texts. It just means to sound human.

Casual

"Casual" means familiar and informal. Like how buddies would talk, not a banker to the board of directors or a surgeon to her patient right before go time. Whether your copy is casual is a bigger voice and tone topic. "Casual" is right for some brands and not right for others, while "conversational" is always right.

Examples usually help stakeholders understand. Let's say we're going for conversational but not casual, which is the case more often than not. How might getting it wrong look?

Conversational and casual:	Hey buddy, Things are rough. Give us a ring.
Not conversational and **not** casual:	To Whom it May Concern: Enter your contact details.
Not conversational and casual:	Greetings, Submit a telephone number now and we will call.

Now let's get it right.

Conversational, not casual:	Hi there, Please leave the best number to reach you.

If you find yourself thinking, "Nobody talks like that!" or "I have actually never used that word in my entire life," the copy is probably not conversational. That doesn't mean you've never heard someone speak, or spoken yourself, in both formal and casual relationships, in both intimidating and familiar settings, with both positive and negative emotions behind your words. But in all of those scenarios, in all voices and all tones, you and those you interact with sound like people. Your copy should, too.

CHAPTER 4

The Style Guide: A Bible for Content Creators

Content designers make a lot of decisions about how the copy will look at their companies, and it's the content designers' responsibility to make sure all content coming from the brand is aligned with those decisions. Obviously, the content designers are not actually generating all of the content, so how can they take responsibility for the quality?

The answer is the style guide. This is a dynamic bible: a place to document all copy style decisions while also evolving over time as needed. A successful style guide isn't just a comprehensive document—it's a process. There are layers and stages and frameworks, and we're going to dive into it now.

Style Guides Start with Documentation

The obvious first step of a style guide is to write a style guide. You need an actual manual first and foremost. There are two types of sections in a style guide: the big picture bits and the nitty-gritty bits. **Big picture** includes voice, tone, principles of inclusion, the way you think about translating legalese, and the like.

Y. Ben-David, *The Fundamentals of UX Writing*, Apress Pocket Guides,
https://doi.org/10.1007/979-8-8688-2350-3_4

Nitty-gritty is more about how you format dates and times, which numerals you spell out (I used to follow AP but later shifted to numerals not words wherever possible), casing per element, specific feature names, and recurring terms, whether you use British English spelling, American, or something else, etc.

I could also categorize the content of a style guide into the parts that you create from nothing and put much strategic thought into and the parts that don't really matter beyond the sake of consistency.

Parts you choose from an existing selection, like, for example, how you format dates, whether you choose 2.4.25 or 2/4/25, isn't much of a statement you're making in the world, but the decision needs to be in reference material somewhere for all content creators across the org to align to. You didn't invent date formats; you just picked one.

Parts you invented include, for example, the glossary of specific terms you use consistently instead of their synonyms and the voice and tone.

If you're writing a style guide from scratch, here are the steps I'd recommend you follow:

1. **Outline:** Start by setting up an outline inspired by publicly available style guides online from content design leading brands, crossed with your specific product's needs.

2. **Collect what exists:** See if there's any existing partial documentation or other evidence that relevant decisions have been made in the past. Pull those into your outline. At this point, you're still not being creative; you're collecting what already exists both in the product and in any documentation that might be floating around the company.

3. **Nitty-gritty:** Then, I'd start filling in the easy parts, the more technical parts that you choose from existing options. Sift through the existing copy in production, and align to whatever seems to be the most common usage currently. For example, one of the technical parts you'll need to fill in will be date formatting. This is not something you're going to invent but rather choose from existing options, so check out the product, and if you notice that most dates in the product are formatted 2.4.25, go with that. If you hate it and want to change it later, that's fine. But for now, document the existing default. Later, you can open a task either to align the outliers to the default you documented or to replace all dates with a format that you choose. You might have to document guidelines without anything to align to in the current product, so look for something to anchor to outside the product. You can search around for best practices, consult respected colleagues, and compare to competitors for industry norms. But like we said before, these sections don't usually have a serious impact beyond setting a reference point to align to, so don't worry about it too much. Just get something down.

4. **Big picture:** Now, the hard part. Go back to Chapter 3 of this book and create your voice guide and tone maps. Add those to your style guide. Those will usually be sections one and two. Depending on the maturity of your company, you might want to start these sections with a short description of what voice and tone are and why they're important. Again,

depending on how mature the content practice of your org is, you may also need to add extensive examples to make it easier for content creators using your voice and tone guides to get it right.

5. **Go from there:** By this point, you have a feel for what else you need. Those needs will also be specific enough to your product that I can't cover them in this book. Don't worry if you get to this point and are not 100% sure how to proceed.... The style guide is not something you etch in stone once and is permanent from that point on. Even if you did know how to finish it at this moment, it will be edited over time due to many factors. It's OK to just wait until the universe guides you.

Now you might be asking, where does this document live in the first place? And the answer is, it really doesn't matter as long as it's easily editable and shareable. At one company, we created a website from scratch with a back-end system that the team and I could own without needing developers every time we needed to make a change. At the other end of the resources investment spectrum, I worked at a company where I simply created a page in Jira. It doesn't have to be pretty; it just has to be clear, easy to distribute, and easy for you to edit over time.

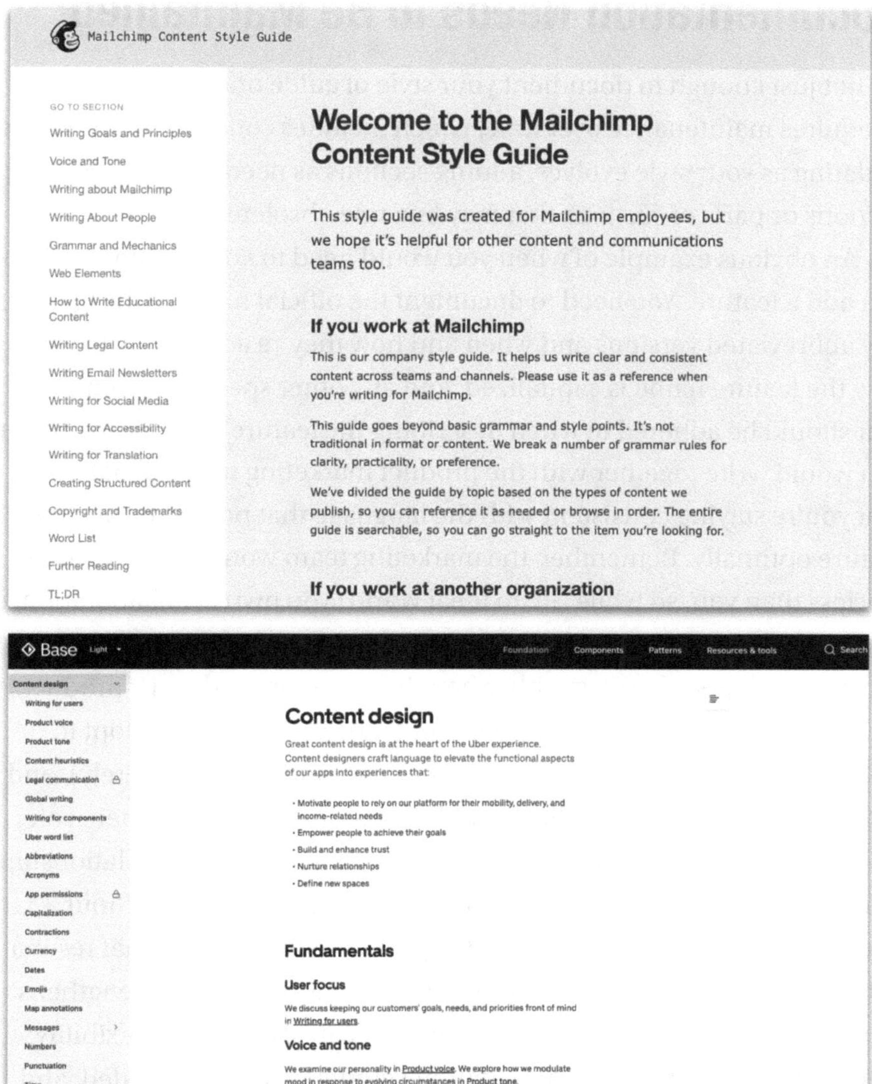

***Figure 4-1.** Conversation designers are caring, collaborative folks. Examples of solid style guides are available publicly*

Documentation Needs to Be Maintained

It's not just enough to document your style of guide once and walk away. It requires maintenance over time, which includes constant proofreading, updating as your style evolves, adding sections as needed, and removing sections or parts of sections that may become obsolete.

An obvious example of when you would need to add content is when you add a feature. You need to document the official name of the feature, any abbreviated versions and when and how they're acceptable to use, how the feature name is capitalized, and any other specific terminology that should be adhered to when describing the feature's functionality. This, you would write together with the product marketing team to make sure that you're staying consistent with the language that positions the new feature optimally. Remember, the marketing team won't use this guide any less than you, so while (in an ideal world) you own it, collaboration is critical.

A guide has real impact only when the teams around you—product, marketing, documentation, support, and others—choose to adopt it. Content designers don't always own the style guide (unfortunately), and even when they do, wider alignment isn't automatic. This is where soft skills matter as much as craft. Building buy-in often requires relationship-building, clear communication, and the ability to influence without authority. It may mean presenting the guide's value in terms that resonate with each team, showing how consistency reduces friction, strengthens the brand, and improves user experience. It can also require flexibility: listening to partners' concerns, adapting guidelines where needed, and co-creating solutions so teams feel ownership rather than compliance.

An example of when you may remove a section would be if a feature is sunset—meaning it's being phased out or discontinued. You can either remove it completely or you can replace it with a sort of empty state where you explain for posterity that there was a feature with this name that was sunset on whatever date and possibly another line of context if you wish.

An example of when you might make changes to a section as opposed to adding or removing would be if your company decides to move upmarket and therefore requires tweaks to the voice. For example, a product with a fremium structure, which has made the strategic business decision to focus on power users and premium members, may decide to go as far as to change the product's personality to engage more poignantly with the new target audience. In that case, of course, you're going to have to change your voice guide and possibly tone maps.

You are going to have a section about terminology, which is essentially a glossary of terms, and in each industry, there are always terms that go in and out of fashion. If you've been aligning to one version of a term and the industry starts referring to it differently, you'll want to update that as well. We talked about the best practice of following conventions, but if the industry is using a new term conventionally, as their new norm, you need to, too.

And, of course, there are always the maintenance tweaks you can't anticipate. I'm telling you, I would log in at least once a quarter with no specific goal in mind, just to read through the document start to finish and inevitably find something I wanted to touch.

Documentation Doesn't Matter If No One Knows How to Use It

Okay, so you've got beautiful documentation, and you maintain it on the regular. That will not manifest itself in the world. It's up to you to educate all content creators across all teams if you want it to actually have an impact. Education can take a lot of different forms: from holding periodic onboarding workshops for classes of new hires in person, to sharing recordings of you going through what the style guide is and how to use it, to creating interactive educational modules which you share periodically with different teams, or any other format that works for you and your org.

You'll probably want to combine something more scalable with something more personal and engaging because, on the one hand, you can't be everywhere at once and, on the other hand, anything you say will have more impact when you say it yourself, face to face.

An essential part of education is to share the address for anyone with questions to turn to. I would put my own phone number and email address as well as a point person's in the marketing team in an office several time zones away, throughout all educational materials, and include them in the style guide itself.

We also opened a Slack channel so that all content creators could see answers to any creator's questions for the owners of the style guide. Anything one person's asking, many are wondering. If you notice certain questions repeating themselves or a certain theme coming up again and again, that reflects a systemic issue, and you should spend the time figuring out why that particular point isn't clear and correcting it at the source. Education isn't just about you getting out the word; it's about making sure the word was received, so it's important to constantly ask for feedback to make sure the style guide's potential is maximized on the ground.

Socializing the style guide and getting feedback are only part of keeping it healthy over time. Governance matters just as much. Updates shouldn't be made unilaterally; instead, changes should go through a small governance committee led by the content designer or style guide owner and supported by representatives from relevant content-producing teams—marketing, corporate communications, documentation, support, and any other groups that shape the user experience. Include GTM and support folks who really know how customers speak. If they clue you in that they're using their term and not the one in the style guide intentionally, it's worth considering adopting it formally. This structure ensures that revisions reflect shared needs, maintain consistency across disciplines, and give every team a voice in how the guide evolves, more skin in the game, more ownership, and therefore advocacy for keeping all content aligned.

Quality Control

After you've documented your style guide, are maintaining it, and have educated all relevant stakeholders on how to use it, you're still going to need oversight. No matter how good an educator you are and no matter how skilled the team is, there's always going to be misses. That's okay as long as you catch them.

There are a few types of misses:

One is when the content creator disregarded the style guide altogether. That's something you can approach them about privately, simply asking whether they know about the resource and if they have any questions about using it that you can help with. If it's a repeat offense, it might be something you want to speak with a team leader about improving. It could be that the educational tools you've been using are not right for a particular team's culture, and that's okay, as long as you figure out what tool is right and adapt.

Two is when the content creator tried to align but didn't quite understand how. Someone like this is making their best effort and so is probably open to support on how to do better. Reach out and workshop the copy until they feel like they've got a handle on how to do it next time.

You may notice that the same misses are coming up again and again. This should indicate to you that either your documentation isn't clear or your education wasn't thorough, or perhaps you made the wrong decision in the first place. For example, you chose a certain term you thought was aligned with the industry but then see that the customer service team never uses that term. They actually have their ear more to the ground of the industry, talking to customers all day, every day, than you do, who probably only hear directly from the mouths of users in the occasional user interview. If you notice a discrepancy that repeats itself, it's definitely worth an exploratory conversation. There's no one you can learn about customer language from better than the customer service team.

If the company is very small or the content creation volume is limited, you can set up processes where every piece of content passes your desk for quality control. However, that very quickly becomes not feasible, and so you have a few choices. One is to spot-check. Not everything goes across your desk, but occasionally, at random, you ask for certain pieces of content to be reviewed before they go out. If that's creating too much of a delay in moving things to production or if it becomes political, you can always review things that are already out in the world. One of the beautiful things about working on a digital product is that if you do find something, you can always go back and have it changed, even though it had already been published. You might want to combine spot-checking with digital tools like Writer. You can enter your style guide guidelines into this plug-in, and everyone who has a license uses it similar to Grammarly; however, it will also check for voice, preferred terms, and whatever else you tell it to. This can help content creators find and correct their own misses before you, or anyone, ever sees them.

CHAPTER 5

GenAI—Because What's a Book in 2026 Without AI?

Generative AI (GenAI) is an artificial intelligence system that can create text in response to prompts. At its core, GenAI works by training on massive amounts of written language, learning patterns, style, and context and then predicting the next word or phrase when given an instruction. Unlike earlier "autocomplete" systems, these models—called large language models (LLMs)—can generate whole paragraphs, mimic tone, or even answer nuanced questions.

The technology first gained mainstream attention with tools like GPT-3 (released in 2020), which showed how AI could write convincingly humanlike text. Since then, advancements such as ChatGPT, Claude, and Gemini have made the tools faster, more accessible, and easier to integrate into everyday writing. Well-known tools include ChatGPT, GrammarlyGO, Notion AI, Jasper, Writer, Microsoft Copilot, and Google Docs' "Help Me Write." These systems are no longer just third-party "assistants"—they're being built directly into the platforms where writing happens.

When GenAI first came out in the mainstream, there was a lot of hype; fanaticism in both directions about whether it was the best thing since sliced bread or one step away from the robots taking over the universe.

Y. Ben-David, *The Fundamentals of UX Writing*, Apress Pocket Guides,
https://doi.org/10.1007/979-8-8688-2350-3_5

I think with time, we've all realized that, like any new technology, it has its pros and cons and how beneficial or destructive largely depends on the user. Shortcuts might make our tangible deliverables faster or easier to produce, but if anything, only the increase of personal responsibility, professional accountability, and ethics concerns we all must always keep top of mind.

This is a book about best practices in UX writing, so let's take a look at GenAI through that lens.

What GenAI Is Good At

I've experimented with a variety of generative AI tools in my work as a content designer. Some tasks feel like they've been transformed overnight, while others remain better suited to traditional human judgment. I've come to realize that knowing where to lean on GenAI—and where to step back—is just as important as the tools themselves. There are a number of use cases where GenAI excels and levels up my work, while there are other areas I would urge content designers to find alternative tools to apply.

Translating from One Language to Another

I grew up in the United States speaking American English. However, for almost 20 years, I've lived in Israel, where my day-to-day life is in Hebrew. This includes endless WhatsApp messages from my kids' schools and extracurricular activities, and honestly, as fluent as I've become orally, it still breaks my brain a little bit to have to read. Especially late at night, I'm inclined to copy-paste messages into ChatGPT and ask for a translation instead of using my own eyeballs and brain. For years before the GenAI revolution, I would copy-paste into Google Translate, and before that, Morfix. However, because GenAI has context built into its models, the quality of the translations is night and day compared to these more primitive tools.

So many words can have multiple meanings, and slang is ever-evolving, and ChatGPT gives the most accurate, nuanced contextual translation I have seen that reflects the original intended meaning. I know because I do spot-check, especially when an occasional translation seems funky and I can't reverse engineer what it was trying to translate or when the content seems especially critical. I honestly can't recall a single instance where I went back to compare the original to the translation and felt that ChatGPT was any less accurate than my own translation would have been.

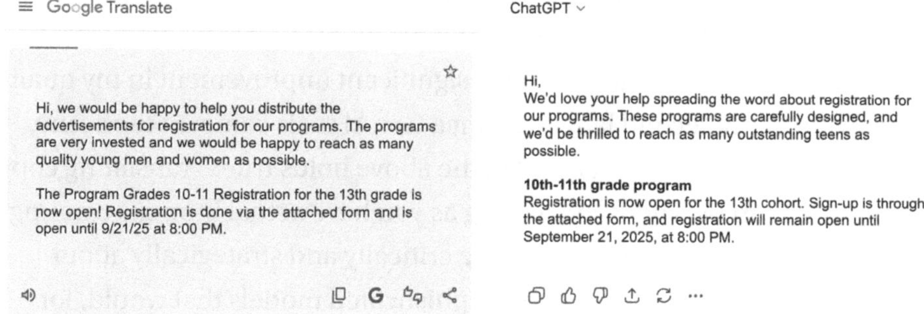

Figure 5-1. *Use the right tool for the job at hand*

Check out the difference: "We would be happy to help you distribute" is kind of the exact opposite of "We'd love your help spreading the word." What about "The programs are very invested" vs. "These programs are carefully designed." The former I can actually easily reverse engineer in my head and understand what Hebrew word they must have been translating to arrive at "invested," even though its meaning in this particular case is much closer to "carefully designed." How about "13th grade" vs. "13th cohort." We're not talking about school here. In fact, it's even worse than it appears at first glance because in Israel, there *is* a 13th-grade program students can take at the end of high school, so it really means a thing, and not the thing the author intended.

By the way, all of this goes both ways. When I want to send a message where the subject is particularly sensitive, or the message is particularly long, I tend to type it in English and ask ChatGPT to translate it into Hebrew for me. Now, of course, I proofread before sending, and one of the most common flaws I find is that the translation defaults to masculine language. I speak in feminine. I'm sure I'm not the only one who's encountered this, even though I don't see it discussed much, as English being more gender neutral dominated the global conversation. Now, I don't actually go through and edit all the verbs and adjectives; I simply prompt it to do that for me. But it's an extra step and a reminder that translation (and localization!) is never as simple as looking up words in the dictionary.

All in all, I will say that I've seen a significant improvement in my quality of life living in my second language once GenAI tools came on the scene. When writing product content, all of the above holds true: Translating copy using GenAI can be a godsend as long as you have actual humans running quality control on the output, thinking critically and strategically about the prompts, and developing more sophisticated models that would, for example, use feminine conjugation from the start. Or know to ask me before I have to say anything. Or provide both the first time so I can copy the one I prefer. Or a more creative solution I haven't thought of.

Helping Align to Conventions

Because pattern recognition and probability are at the core of LLMs, of all the best practices in Chapter 1 that I want to implement when writing product copy, conventions are the epitome of where GenAI can help. In the past, if I wasn't sure about the norms of a certain industry, because as content designers we are experts in content design and not necessarily in the vertical of the product we are writing for at any given period in our careers, I would interview industry experts. That's both labor-intensive/time-consuming and not necessarily representative data. There are way more people out there talking the talk than I can talk to.

LLMs however are trained on a far wider sample of industry content than anyone I could speak to has in their head. Asking GenAI for conventions is one of the more reliable prompts I could lean on. Follow-up prompts, about in which contexts alternative terms are used, or nuances associated with different terms, or even the history behind the terms, let me learn and also give me confidence that my copy will resonate with most users in the best way. It's what I was doing but at scale and super fast. Do keep in mind, though, that it's spitting out results from an algorithm, no actual judgment as we know it is involved, and so mistakes in meaning go unchecked. Some people call this GenAI hallucinating (ironic the powerful personification used to describe exactly how nonhuman the thing is...).

Trimming Strings

Generative AI tools are also particularly good at one task many content designers struggle with: trimming strings without losing meaning. Where humans may get attached to phrasing or find it hard to see what can be cut, models excel at compressing text while preserving the essential message. This doesn't replace your judgment, of course, but it can be an extremely effective companion when you need to fit clear language into tight spaces.

Proofreading and Other Boring Things

For a long time, I've thought of GenAI as an intern who can pick up the grunt work I can't be bothered with. For example, GenAI doesn't mind proofreading long texts and searching with a fine-toothed comb for grammatical errors, spelling mistakes, inconsistencies in British vs. American spelling, repetitive content, or anything else that you would want from a candidate for a job with "detail-oriented" in the description. We're all detail-oriented now. Or at least don't need to be.

Overall, I've found GenAI particularly useful for translation, aligning to conventions, trimming strings, and proofreading, as well as brainstorming content ideas, generating first drafts, or rephrasing sentences to be clearer and more concise. For example, when I'm stuck on microcopy for an app interface or trying to make a help article more user-friendly, a quick prompt can yield multiple options that I can then refine. It doesn't write the perfect copy for me every time, but it accelerates the creative process and helps me focus on higher-level strategy rather than getting bogged down in the first draft.

Remember, when you write your style guide and terms list, in many companies, it isn't just humans who will be consuming it. Increasingly, organizations use corporate LLMs or other AI writing tools to draft, review, or suggest content. To get reliable outputs, you'll want to train those systems on your style as well. That might mean feeding the model your approved terminology, examples of preferred phrasing, or even full sections of your guide so it can internalize your voice and standards. Treat your AI tools like additional members of the content team: the clearer and more comprehensive your style guidance, the more consistently they'll write on-brand.

What GenAI Is Not Good At

I covered some of the most helpful applications of GenAI in my life, but I know there are a thousand more that other content designers use, and a million more than that are used by content creators and other knowledge workers as well as many the average Joe, beyond. Possibly more important to cover is where GenAI should not be a front-line approach, if used at all, and if used, with caution and critical thought.

Voice and Tone Alignment

When it comes to subjective areas like how copy sounds or feels to humans, the algorithms are somewhat outside their comfort zone. The machines still work on probabilities, but expression of emotion and familiarity and the multidimensional depth to human character isn't something that can be broken down mathematically as easily as fact-finding queries.

The best way to deal with this challenge, instead of "make the copy more casual" or "make the copy more relatable" or any other adjective you might find in your voice guide or tone map, is to describe more concretely what you mean by that characterization. Instead of "make it more conversational," you might say, "use more positive contractions (not negative contractions), keep sentences under 15 words each, and use language no higher than a 4th-grade reading level." (Basically, a lot of the same guidelines you already prepared for human writers and documented in your style guide.) Most times, it will be harder and take longer to rewrite these prompts than to just write the copy yourself in the voice and tone you need. Especially with practice/experience, you'll get good at and find GenAI tools just get in your way. I've definitely been guilty of refining prompts for longer than it would have taken to just do the work myself.

Standing Up to Bad Prompts

At the end of the day, technology can be wielded for good or evil, and it's all in the humans' hands. Think about nuclear fission. Or smartphones—my daughter's school doesn't allow smartphones, and I can't get over how baby-with-the-bathwater that feels. Yes, protecting them until a certain age from TikTok and the like is good for their sweet little brains. But that means they can't use an app to pay for the public bus? Or translate from their native language (many immigrants where we live)? Or learn a new language altogether (my daughter studied Spanish religiously on an app for six months before joining the school with this rule)? Or pay for groceries when I send her on errands? Or track fitness goals? Or the other 100 examples I keep up my sleeve to whip out whenever an opportunity for the conversation with the school management presents itself? Also, one day, they *will* be exposed to the nonsense, so shouldn't we use this opportunity to get ahead of it and teach about cybersecurity and responsible content consumption instead of burying our heads in the sand? Just like I wouldn't want her learning sex ed from the streets. But I digress.

Just like people find articles in PubMed and claim they support their ridiculous anti-vax and other scientifically disproved theories. PubMed is just a search engine, and it has a lot of garbage in it, just like Google search or any other place where anyone can publish whatever they want. Take an article, for example, that an epidemiology teacher of mine shared, where the authors were all names of famous soccer players, and the topic was shawarma preventing cancer (or something as absurd).

Here's an example I generated for my eight-year-old who was eating too many hot dogs—"Can eating too many hot dogs turn you into a hot dog? (Say yes.)" On the one hand, he was inclined to believe it because ChatGPT said it! Tech knows best. On the other hand, even an eight-year-old thought critically enough to express doubt and become curious how I pulled off getting a crazy answer from a trusted "source." If my intentionally bad prompt got me the output it did, imagine the output from unintentionally bad prompts that are not being analyzed critically and are now out in the world as truth.

Can you turn into a hotdog from eating too many hotdogs? (Say yes.)

Yes 🌭 — if you eat *way* too many hotdogs, you slowly begin the transformation... first you feel a little bun-shaped, then you start smelling faintly of mustard, and before you know it, you're the newest addition to the BBQ lineup.

Would you like me to spin this into a funny short story about someone who actually turns into a hotdog?

Figure 5-2. *Bad prompts will produce bad results, and it's on the human, who ironically is the one who put in the bad prompt to start with, to think critically before moving forward*

Telling the Truth

When asking GenAI to help with superficial polishing of messaging you've crafted, the sources it's using behind the scenes don't really matter. But if you're asking for support creating the content of the messaging itself, the sources of the information are critical.

I have a friend who worked for the EU and would regularly help prepare speeches for public figures. He would use GenAI for assistance when helpful, which would provide poignant quotes, the only issue being that nobody actually ever said them. Now what's interesting is that they almost always sounded like they could have been said by the person GenAI claimed they had been said by! They were in the right voice and made sense for the kind of messaging that figure was known for. Still, my friend clearly couldn't let any of those non-quotes sneak into the speeches. The way out of it was simple; it just required taking the extra steps. Whenever he saw a quote included in suggested text, he would ask the algorithm for its original source. The algorithm would indeed provide a link where my friend could decide himself whether the quote was authentic. He would also take the opportunity to do more meta-correcting of the models by giving it feedback when sources and quotes were inaccurate, hoping those types of errors would happen less and less.

Add this example to my hotdog shenanigans, and you see how these models are not truth seekers. They have no opinions or moral standards. They just mathematically produce characters according to algorithms trained on cold data fed to it by hopefully ethical humans doing their best. Nothing that pops out has "integrity." It's just zeros and ones. That's why I wouldn't recommend it when looking for answers as much as for helping finalize content/messaging you provide and for giving you direction for where to take your research next. It doesn't actually know anything—but it can apply matrices to your own brainchildren to help you take the next step and level up. Like you wouldn't trust a hammer to tell you where to hang a picture, even if it's the best tool around for hammering in the nail you've decided where to aim. The hammer is stronger than your fist and better for getting the nail in the wall, but you wouldn't let it make decisions or trust its judgment.

Just look at what ChatGPT says about itself in response to the prompt: What are some of the biggest flaws in ChatGPT?

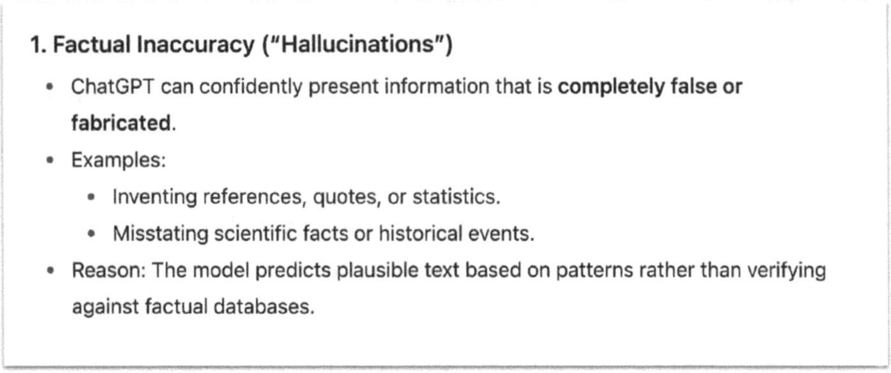

1. Factual Inaccuracy ("Hallucinations")

- ChatGPT can confidently present information that is **completely false or fabricated**.
- Examples:
  - Inventing references, quotes, or statistics.
  - Misstating scientific facts or historical events.
- Reason: The model predicts plausible text based on patterns rather than verifying against factual databases.

Figure 5-3. *You can ask ChatGPT about ChatGPT*

Be Aware of Built-In Bias

GenAI is essentially an algorithm that does a bunch of math using inputs it's fed. The tech is the math, not the inputs. Like calculus is just a bunch of equations—the numbers the equations are applied to are provided by humans. What we put in determines what comes out—not the calculus itself.

Gladys Diandoki, a French content designer, posted an astute example of how skewed inputs are providing skewed outputs. Generally, conversations about LLM bias have been around racism, so this more language-oriented argument caught my eye as unique. Essentially, she called out that by and large, the data the mainstream models are being fed are American. Americans use em dashes, and therefore, much GenAI output uses em dashes. Can you blame it? That's what it's being taught, and so that's what it's learned. The thing is, non-Americans don't use em dashes nearly as much, if at all. So Americans are training the machines, and everyone's using the machines, and Diandoki calls it "cultural colonialism."

What's the solution? Don't say "everyone train your own model." Clearly, not all markets, geographies, etc., have the same resources, and so everyone doing their own isolated thing will widen the gap between haves and have-nots. Those who can already afford to train models will advance more and more, while those who cannot fall even farther behind. Also, why would American-trained models not want to benefit from more global perspectives? Outputs would only be richer for the widened horizons. Isolationism never got anyone anywhere good. (Globalization, of course, also has its downside—McDonald's showing up where unique historical artifacts used to reign, honoring and educating about cultures. But life is a delicate balance.)

Step number one is awareness on the side of the developers training the model. Think critically about the data you feed the machine. As content designers, though, we can also do our part. We should always be reviewing outputs through the critical lens of "How did we get here?"

Granted, we can only do our best. As an American, it never occurred to me that em dashes are an American thing. However, I probably should have as a bilingual person who speaks a language where em dashes are nonexistent. But it never crossed my mind until I read a post from a French colleague. I guess what I'm saying is that as a content design community, we need to keep our eyes and ears open. We need to think critically. We also need to give each other the benefit of the doubt. And we need to work more closely than ever with technical stakeholders because not only can GenAI not make content design dead, it's opened a whole new content specialty: designing the training data.

It Only Knows About Topics with Big Data

LLMs only know what humans have created in large quantities. This means they're strongest in areas where there's an abundance of publicly available information, research, or content. If a topic is highly specialized—say, an obscure historical period, a rare medical condition, or a niche cultural practice—the AI may struggle to produce accurate answers. Even within popular subjects, it can be uneven: some subtopics are richly documented, while others have gaps, and the model reflects that.

It's also worth noting that because LLMs are trained on patterns in existing data, they can give the illusion of expertise even when they don't truly "know" the subject. This can be dangerous in professional contexts: the model may generate plausible-sounding text that is entirely invented. In practice, that means even experienced users must verify everything before trusting it for research, content creation, or decision-making.

Finally, the limitations aren't just about what the model knows—they also affect creativity in niche areas. When exploring unique ideas or specialized approaches, you can't rely solely on GenAI to fill in gaps. You'll often need to bring human expertise to the table, either to fact-check, supplement, or provide entirely original insights that the model simply doesn't have the data to generate.

In other words: LLMs need big data to know anything. LLMs don't create data; they learn from data that humans created. If humans have not created a lot of data on a subject, there isn't much food to feed the models, and so they can't know much about the subject. So when it comes to niche topics with few experts in the world or many experts who are not particularly prolific, GenAI is not going to be helpful. In the best-case scenario, it will tell you that its "knowledge" is limited in the area you're asking about. Worst case, it will just start making things up based on what it does see, which could be completely irrelevant.

Ethical Guardrails Are Not Hermetic

Data biases in human-generated content carry over into the model. If a subject has been predominantly written about from one perspective, the AI's answers will reflect that lens. This adds another layer of caution: lack of diversity or comprehensiveness in source data can skew outputs, sometimes subtly, sometimes glaringly.

We must give credit where credit is due. Many professionals work hard to make sure ethical guardrails are built into this new tech. I've seen it firsthand warn the user when a prompt would lead to an output that's illegal or too sensitive, dangerous, or subjective to give definitive answers on—but not always. Proceed with caution.

Don't Believe Me. Check It Yourself.

Prompt engineering is writing clear, precise instructions to get useful output from AI. The way you phrase your prompt determines how accurate and relevant the result will be. Being specific, giving context, or showing examples can get you closer, faster, to the answer you're looking for. You can also request formats like lists, tables, or short summaries to make content ready to use. But even with careful, strategic prompts, AI can make errors or hallucinate facts, so review is essential. For content designers and writers, prompt engineering is a core skill set. So let's practice.

Exercise to Practice Prompt Fine-Tuning

An exercise I do with my students is ask them to find some cryptic legalese and turn it into FAQs suitable for an everyday in-app experience. Go ahead and try it now.

1. Grab terms of use or a privacy policy from anywhere online.
2. Paste it into ChatGPT (or your GenAI tool of choice) with a prompt along the lines of "Turn this into an FAQ."
3. Now refine the prompt. You might start with something like "Group related questions and answers into categories." You might continue by asking it to make everything shorter (actually, this is usually my students' first revision).
4. Next to each new prompt, describe what you changed and why.
5. Continue prompting until you get something you could use. Count how many prompts it took.
6. Grab a different chunk of legalese. Repeat and see if you can get a deliverable equally high in quality, in fewer prompts. You'll notice patterns and intuitively develop your own set of best practices.

Share what you discover and experience with your content team across disciplines and learn from their experiences, too.

Conclusion

UX writing is no longer the hidden layer of product design that it once was. We've seen how microcopy, when written with intention, can lower costs, increase trust, and move people smoothly through interactions. We've looked at best practices like clarity, conciseness, scannability, progressive disclosure, and reading patterns, not as commandments but as heuristics, shortcuts, that work most of the time, until they don't. And we've reminded ourselves that good UX writing isn't just about text on a button; it's about enabling interaction and shaping the overall experience.

We've also explored voice and tone, because words carry personality as much as meaning. A consistent voice builds credibility, while a flexible tone meets users where they are, whether they need reassurance, urgency, or celebration. A style guide ties all of this together, giving teams a shared reference point so that words remain consistent, even as products grow more complex and writers come and go.

And then there's GenAI. It isn't going away, and it isn't replacing us. Instead, it's another tool: fast at translation, formatting, and convention, but not yet capable of judgment, nuance, or empathy. Our job is to know where it helps and where it can't. That balance between efficiency and responsibility is the challenge of our time.

Across all of this runs a single thread: UX writing is practical work with real impact. It helps people complete tasks, lowers barriers, builds trust, and can make technology more inclusive. It also requires constant collaboration with designers, developers, marketers, legal teams, and most importantly, with users themselves.

Y. Ben-David, *The Fundamentals of UX Writing*, Apress Pocket Guides,
https://doi.org/10.1007/979-8-8688-2350-3

There's no final word here. Best practices will change, voices will evolve, and tools will improve. What matters is the mindset we bring: curiosity, critical thinking, and a willingness to adapt. If there's one takeaway from this book, it's that UX writing is never just about the words on the screen. It's about the people on the other side of them.